THE WILL TO WIN

THE CURT BRINKMAN STORY

KEITH J. KARREN

RANDALL BOOK CO.

DEDICATION

To the two very special people who helped make this success story happen, Raymond and Karma Brinkman, and to our inspirations, Bonnie and Diane, whose support and love have allowed us to live purposefully.

ISBN 0–934126–18–6

Third Printing February 1987

Randall Book Company
1182 N. Industrial Park Drive
Orem, UT 84057

Printed in the United States of America

CONTENTS

CHAPTER 1
Tragedy

Like something out of a nightmare, the old ambulance sped off the main road of the Idaho countryside and across the fields, its wailing siren piercing the stillness of the morning air. People had often laughed at the paradox the old hearse-turned-ambulance portrayed, but there was no laughing now. It was coming for one of *them*! Only in a dream would a hearse be so out of place, careening through the half light of the early morning, floundering across the summer fields. But this was no dream, and perhaps that was the worst part of it; no waking would dispell the horror of the morning or undo what had happened.

Trying desperately to reach the pumphouse, the ambulance bounced over the potato furrows, creating clouds of dust that could be seen for miles. It shot over a ditch, swerving recklessly to avoid overturning. Every second counted, and the driver sweat nervously.

After what seemed like an eternity, the old vehicle crossed the last wide ditch and raced up the hill to where the small crowd had gathered. As the orderlies lifted the torn, yet incredibly alive young Curtis Brinkman into the ambulance, every jolt brought cries of excruciating pain. With only oxygen to give him, they put the mask on him half in hopes that it would help and half to stop his screaming. Passing in and out of a painful fog, not quite conscious, but not quite gone, he kept thinking, "I didn't mean it, I didn't mean it," but didn't really know what he meant.

Curtis began to fade, shock making him oblivious to almost everything; it was a blessing. How many hours — or maybe weeks or years — had gone by since the whole thing had begun?

It was July 6, 1970, about 4:30 in the morning. Curtis, then sixteen, and his thirteen year old brother, Greg, were moving pipe like they did every summer, and their days started early. Getting up and waking up are two different things at that time of the morning, so when the boys dragged themselves outside and realized their ride was late, they just curled up on the porch and went back to sleep.

Suddenly, somebody was "laying on" the horn, and there was the old '56 station wagon, filled with the crew, impatient because they were so late getting started. Curtis and Greg jumped up and reached for their gear only to find they hadn't taken it out of the garage yet. All of their work clothes were kept out there in a box — the boots, gloves, sweatshirts, and the rubber aprons they had to wear to keep the wet off their legs when they moved the pipe. They grabbed everything and hurried back out to the car, tumbled into the back, and fell asleep again.

After arriving at the farm and because everyone was so tired, they decided to take a nap before starting work. The crew of seven boys, Curtis being the oldest, had worked for Jay Stalworthy several summers now, so Jay knew them well and was never shocked at some of the crazy things like this that the boys did.

When Curtis finally woke up, it was about 6:30. He started sorting through the gear he had grabbed in the garage and found two right boots instead of one completed pair. The thought of running around in the cold and wet with only one boot wasn't pleasant, but going all the way home for the other one was worse, so he just put three socks on his left foot and hoped they'd take the place of the missing boot. One of the straps that was supposed to be keeping his apron tight against his legs had broken, and the whole thing was flapping around loose. That wasn't important, so he pulled on his red sweatshirt and headed toward the sprinklers.

The pipe he was moving was a line of thirty-three, forty-foot sections coming off the mainline, then down through the field. Each section weighed about forty pounds and was bisected by a two foot riser that supported a rainbird sprinklerhead. Each one of those sections had to be disconnected, hefted, carried about forty feet, set down, and reconnected. So, moving a line wasn't easy; however, Curtis had been doing it every summer since seventh grade; he knew the tricks. So, in order to keep it interesting and challenging, they raced the other members of the crew to see who could finish his particular line first.

Curtis was a competitor and got a real kick out of those little contests. He looked forward to the real ones he'd get into in high school. Curtis was going to be a pro basketball player and planned to be the best. He was 6'7" by the time he was sixteen, and things were looking very bright for the future, but this morning he was still a pipe mover, and the only contest was seeing if he could stand moving a whole line in one boot.

The ground was wet. That early in the season, before the spuds had grown vines, the ground tended to get muddy very quickly, so, before getting half way through his line, Curtis was shin deep in mud. Taking the first step into the mess, he lost all three of his socks at once and was left with one bare, cold foot. Next, he cut his big toe on a rock, and it started bleeding. Sinking deeper into the mud with every step taken, he finally finished his line long before anyone else and wanted to go home.

Tony was working the same field, so Curtis went over to help him finish. "Hey," he said, "let's go get the rest of the guys and go home. We can finish the rest this afternoon." Tony had no problem with that at all, so they did the last few sections and headed over to check the pump. Curtis cut his foot some more by walking on the stubble that had been left after the first hay cutting. It was like walking on toothpicks and didn't make things any more comfortable.

The pump was cast iron, about four feet in diameter and six or seven feet high. It was a conglomeration of gauges, valves, and gates, and the crew had to keep their eye on it to make sure the oil levels were okay and the water was going through like it should. The pump was powered by a high voltage line that came down from a pole that stood on the crown of the hill, up behind the pump. That pole was the very end of the power lines, situated

about as far out into the boondocks as it would get. Three
transformers were fastened up at the top of the pole, about
twenty feet above the ground. They looked big, even from the
ground. Three feet in diameter — and dangerous.

Tony and Curtis were just going to check the pump, then
round everybody else up, but by the time they got to the pump,
Curtis didn't feel like hiking around barefoot anymore. When
trying later to remember what had given him the urge to climb
the power pole, all he could recall was Tony saying he was crazy
and then taking off to help his own brother, Jeff, who was
working just over the hill from the pump.

Curtis stood around waiting for awhile but was getting
impatient because his foot was really bothering him. Looking up
at the pole, he wondered if he really could climb it or even
should. He walked up the hill towards it, casually measuring the
distance from the ground to the first toe hold. Finally, standing
right beneath it, Curtis had to stretch his neck way back to see the
top of it. The little glass insulators high in the wires sparkled with
moisture in the first rays of sunlight.

Curtis shifted his gaze, making a swift survey of the land
around, but he couldn't see much because of the hill. He
remembered wanting to go home. I wonder what they're all
doing he thought to himself. He was thinking that he might be
able to help somebody and speed things up a little. With no desire
to take another long hike in those slimy, rocky fields in his
condition, he looked up at the pole again, his mind racing, "If I *did*
climb up there, I could see pretty much where everybody is."

He reached up experimentally. The first hold was still out of
reach by a few inches, tall as he was. Looking around again, he
saw Tony about thirty yards away still walking up the hill
towards his brother Jeff. Curtis reached up again, and this time he
put a little jump behind the reach. The distance was enough so
that he could grasp a hold and pull himself up until he was
securely there. He looked back down at the ground and felt that
feeling of pride a person gets when he has done something hardly
anyone else can do. He just stayed there for awhile, enjoying the

fact that he was so tall and thinking about how he would really knock them out next year in basketball. Then he started to climb.

About half way up, Curtis looked down at the pump and thought that he'd better not fall on that, or he'd be a "dead duck." Peering around the pole to the other side where a swampy area lay, he thought about the tadpoles that were in the water down there. About three weeks ago, he and his buddies had fished around in that run-off for the tadpoles, had taken a bunch of them home, and let them go in Curtis' folks' fish pond. Looking up, he saw how close the transformers were — there were the big cross-members just above the mainline where he could sit for awhile. That'd put him about twenty feet up, enough to see almost everything for miles.

As he climbed up past the transformers, Curtis proceeded cautiously. His apron was flapping around where the strap was broken. Because it was wet, he was trying to stay clear of the lines — he knew they were dangerous. "Careful, Curtis," he said to himself, "you hit those and zap, you've had it." But it wasn't as though he really believed it. He was just like everyone else; no one thinks anything will ever happen to them. He climbed up above the transformers and stopped to look out over the majestic view. His friends looked like little toy men in a Fisher-Price farmyard set.

He was more than twenty feet up with the pump right below him. Holding on to the pole with both hands, he suddenly felt very high. The wind began to blow a little. The power mainline came down near his knees, connecting with the transformers — that's where the arc came from. Whether the apron had blown out and touched the wires or whether the power had just jumped of its own accord no one would ever know. The gentle scene was suddenly shattered by a loud, electrical buzz, brilliantly flashing white light, the explosive sound of ripping flesh and bone and loud, terrifying screams. Three times the white arc attacked Curtis' convulsing body, burning flesh and blowing out bone, causing muscles to contract fearfully, and stopping life in its tracks. Somewhere between

12,000 and 36,000 volts jumped from that line, lancing its way
into Curtis' body, lighting him up like a neon sign. Remembering
it later, all he could think of was that he felt like one of those
cartoon characters who stick their fingers into light sockets and
get all zapped out and stiff, like lightning. His hands fused to the
pole. The breaker didn't disconnect the way it should have, and
the power just kept coming. It got him at the knees and blew
them apart. Burning right through him, it entered somewhere
near his groin and tore through his leg, making an exit for itself
by burning a hole two inches in diameter through his bare left
foot. Then it stopped. Finally the circuit breaker acted, cutting
out the surging power for miles around. The young, lifeless body
slowly toppled from the cross braces. It seemed that God directed
that lifeless body away from the pump below and toward a
water-filled, muddy swamp. Curtis' body slammed into the
swamp with a whoosh. Water bubbled and sizzled as though a
hot poker had been thrust into it.

The shock had killed him. That's what they would tell him
later, but the fall into the cold water miraculously started his heart
again.

Mark Landon — they called him Smash then — saw it from
his line. Later, he would tell Curtis, "I was about halfway through
my line, and I looked up and saw somebody up there in the lines,
and all of a sudden I saw some really bright flashes of light. It
must have happened twice or even three times. I saw these
flashes! Just right there! Then I saw a body and a red T-shirt fall. I
knew it was Curt because he was the only one with a red T-shirt. I
just started running. I ran right past Jeff — right past him. I was
flying right over that hill. Tony was walking around with his
head in his hands. He is Jeff's older brother. Fillmore came later. I
don't know how he heard. Tony was walking around just saying,
'I told him not to go up.' Curt was face down in a big puddle of
water, and I reached down and turned him over. I looked down at
his legs, and his knees were both completely gone. Blown away.
It was white. I remember there was no blood, but it really stunk
of burnt human flesh. It smelled bad. We turned him over

because he couldn't breathe in the water."

Curtis was sizzling like a steak under the broiler, and the water around him was steaming. The boys were running into each other in the confusion, and it might have been funny if it hadn't been so utterly tragic. They tried to move him out of the water, but every time they touched him, Curtis screamed with pain, and it frightened them so badly that they ended up leaving him there. Actually, the water was what saved his life; it retarded the burning process and kept him from literally cooking right through.

Curtis was in shock. He was partly conscious, enough to look down at his knees and see the white bones sticking out of the charred flesh. The kneecap was gone — they never would find it. Curtis knew he was in trouble. He said out loud, "I'll never walk again," and then cried. He screamed, then cried, then said over and over again that he was sorry, he was sorry. Then he'd fall into dead silence. The boys covered him with every bit of clothing they had outside of pants and boots, trying to comfort him, trying to do the best thing. He kept screaming. But that was almost easier on them than the periods of quiet.

Smash Landon remembered: "We were all sitting around waiting. There was nothing we could do. I remember Curtis screaming because he was in pain. He was out of his head — in shock screaming 'Kill me! Kill me!' So I reached down there and slugged him. I had to slap him out of it. I'd slap him a minute, and then he'd get back into it again. I couldn't stand it. My bud's lying down there just dying, and I'm sure he didn't realize what he was saying. I just slapped him. Those guys, my buddies, wondered what I was doing. I go, 'He can't say that.' So we all sat around, and we started praying."

A couple of boys finally went to get Jay, the boss. When he arrived, he knelt down in the mud next to Curtis and checked things out the best he could. It made him sick inside, but somebody had to take care of things, and it looked like he was the only one who could still think. Jay sent someone to call an ambulance and sent a couple of other boys to tell Curtis' mother.

He cautioned them not to sound scared or tell her what happened because they didn't really know how bad it was yet and didn't want to scare her to death.

Jay looked down at Curtis. They couldn't just wait there. That was the worst part, not being able to *do* anything. Jay had only been an active Mormon for a year. Just the Sunday before he had been ordained as an elder . . . so he held the Melchizedek Priesthood. He was feeling that power, now realizing there was something very important here to do. He wasn't really sure how to give anybody a blessing; he'd never done it before. But he knew he had the right to do it, and this was an important thing. Jay bent down in the mud and knelt close to Curtis' ear. He wanted to be sure Curtis knew what was happening.

Jay put his hands on Curtis' muddy head and groped for something to say. All he could come up with was the Lord's Prayer, so he said as much of that as he could remember. Then he just told Curtis that everything would be all right, that he would live until he could get help. It wasn't the most beautiful blessing, but there was power in it. Curtis lived!

When the ambulance finally got there, it turned out to be Mr. Nalder with his old hearse-ambulance. There was really no easy way to get the vehicle in to where the boys were. Mr. Nalder had to take it up around through one of the fields, down a little road, and over a big ditch.

By the time he reached Curtis, there was a crowd around the pump. Jay's dad was there; also Mr. Kelley, a farmer who had seen the tragedy happen from his own place, and another farmer who was trying to find out why he'd lost his electrical power.

Mr. Nalder and his assistant made their way through the group. Curtis' legs were bandaged, amid screams and protests. He was transported from the muddy water to the waiting Gerney stretcher, then carefully placed inside the ambulance. An oxygen mask was placed over his still screaming mouth as Jay's dad jumped in to ride with him.

The ambulance slowly moved from the field and onto the country road. The silent group was left behind, still unbelieving the tragic turn of events, watching the ever-dimishing cloud of dust from the speeding ambulance as it finally disappeared. Then they all looked at each other, and one pipe-changer began to cry.

It was a twenty mile trip to Idaho Falls. At first, Curtis kept saying in a muffled sound through the oxygen mask, "I'm sorry, I'm sorry," like that could change anything. Then he lapsed into unconsciousness, his mind taking him far away from the accident.

Curtis was seeing Greg. Greg was three again, somehow, and he was running. There was the feeling that they were doing something wrong. Yes, and Curtis was running, too, and they were laughing. They were laughing because Grandpa had told them not to leave the yard, but they had escaped, and now they were down by the canal where the banks were all grassy. Suddenly, the bank gave way, and Greg disappeared. Curtis threw himself down on the grass where he could see into the canal and saw Greg was too far away, being swept away downstream. Curtis jumped up and ran alongside the canal, hollering and holding out his hand, but he couldn't seem to get any nearer, and couldn't move fast enough, and there was Greg, all the time paddling like crazy. Then Curtis knew the bridge was coming; he knew about it before he saw it — maybe because the water sounds had grown so loud. But he couldn't shake the feeling that he'd been through all of this some other time, and he knew what was going to happen. Then there was the bridge — it was built so the traffic could get over the canal. There was a little hole that went underneath it so Greg could make it to the other side all right, but Curtis got the feeling that once Greg disappeared into that dark little tunnel, he would never get out again, so he hollered again and again at Greg, all the time wondering why they didn't listen to Grandpa. If they hadn't done what they weren't supposed to in the first place, none of this would have happened. Now there was Greg and that bridge. All of a sudden Greg had grabbed onto the grass, or maybe he had hit a shallow place, and was pulling himself out. Curtis was thinking that if he could just get him dried off, everything would be all right again, just like it was before. . . .

There was a jolt; something woke him up. He thought he had just been dreaming. The sweet feeling that everything would be all right still hovered in his mind, and he held it close, clinging to the memory of it. There was another jolt and a flash of pain. He opened his eyes, and all the people were leaning over him, people pulling the stretcher out of the ambulance, and the sight of them reminded him of what had happened, of the shape he was in, of what he had seen of his legs. Then he knew that nothing was all right and that nothing would ever be the same again.

Curtis' father was alone at the hospital. Mrs. Brinkman had phoned her husband and told him to meet Curtis there. She'd told him what the boy on the phone had said: it was nothing serious — maybe just a broken leg. She would meet them later. The hospital wasn't far from his office at the school district, so it had only been a small wait until the ambulance finally got there. He wasn't at all prepared for the reality of the situation.

Curtis' mother was just leaving for the hospital when the boys dropped by on their way there. That was when she finally knew. She could tell that something horrible had happened by the look on their faces.

There was a pile of muddy clothes on the emergency room floor where the staff had stripped Curtis down to expose his demolished form, a hard, cold fact that the boys in the waiting room kept having to come to terms with, over and over as they sat there. Curtis' parents came in together. They were crying. The sight of that kind of grief, adult and quiet as it was, made the boys feel even stranger.

Hospitals are uncomfortable places at the best of times for people who are unfamiliar with them. Waiting in the emergency room, especially at the worst of times, is a special kind of turmoil. The hardest part of the waiting is imagining — how serious could it be? What would we do if he died? How will things be if he lives? And hope is at once a blessing and a torture. Faith is the only comfort, and that holds no promise at all, at least, no temporal one.

The Brinkmans knew their son was alive. That's all they

knew. But they couldn't even be certain of that from one moment to the next. It was a relief when Dr. Davis, the family doctor, finally got a moment to speak with them. He told them that he had called in Dr. Bjorenson, an orthopedic specialist. Dr. Davis had been at a loss as to how to help Curtis, so he was trusting the specialist, and he hoped that the Brinkmans could do the same. Dr. Bjorenson was straight with them; he didn't know how to handle things either. The Idaho Falls hospital just didn't have the facilities. "We can't even touch it," he said. "There's nothing we can do for him. We could cut his legs off, but that may not be the answer at all. Let's send him to Salt Lake. There's a top plastic surgeon in Salt Lake, T. R. Broadbent."

All the hospital really had been able to do for Curtis was clean him up a little. When they wheeled him back out again, the boys who were still waiting had been sitting less than an hour. It had seemed like such a long time for being such a short time. And this was only the beginning.

CHAPTER TWO
Fight for Life

Curtis felt the pressure mostly in his temples and his chest. He struggled to open his eyes, to see through the tremendous pain and confusion in his mind. He was still on his back, and he saw tiny spots above him that finally resolved themselves into something like the roof of a car. He turned his head and felt his body start to scream. He saw an instrument panel, his mother's face, and then the doctor's — he had to be a doctor because he was dressed all in white, and his face was very close. Through his own screaming, Curtis could hear the doctor saying, "It's all right. We're in a plane. We're going to take you to Salt Lake where you'll be all right. Your mother's here." Curtis didn't even feel the needle.

Greg was there again, only he was older now, only not quite old enough still. He was running again, and so was Curtis. They were running down to the river. When Curtis ran up over the crown of the hill and started down the long bank towards the water, he felt like he was doing a long, slow leap, like flying in slow motion. He could see the water, running lazily along, drifting near the bank, swifter towards the middle, and when he looked up, he could see the hazy green canopy of cottonwoods. . .so, so high against the blue sky.

Curtis could see Greg down by the lean-to. It was the best lean-to anybody ever saw. They'd built it up around a big cottonwood, with real corner posts and everything. They used willows for the walls and the roof, willows with the leaves still on so it was really dark inside. There was only one door, and the whole thing was just beautiful the way it was put

*together. It was just great, just great. They had gathered
alfalfa from a nearby hayfield for the floor, and it smelled
sweet — it was deep and dark inside.*

*Now the scene shifted, and they were using a chemistry
set to build a rocket. Curtis couldn't have been any more than
twelve. Everyone could feel the excitement. They were going to
launch it with some fuel they'd made, and everybody was around
close, wanting to see what would happen when it took off.
Somebody said, "Watch out," but the explosion came too fast,
and suddenly it felt like something was burning Curt's left eye
out. Flashes of light shot through his eye and there was pain —
incredible pain. And then he couldn't see. He knew his eye was
open, but he couldn't see. He was in the hospital; they were
bandaging both of his eyes, and he really couldn't see. "You're
lucky," somebody was saying. "For you it'll only be a week.
Some people are blind forever." But he still tried to open his
eyes, and the pain was still there, still awful. . .*

Curtis woke up vomiting. He screamed through his
vomiting, and he could hear his mother making noises like she
was hurt, too. "I'm sorry, I'm sorry," he tried to say, and then he
saw the flash of the needle; this time he felt it.

*He was running again. He was so tired of running. It
was like ninth grade, and there were all these guys running with
him; it seemed like there was a long way to go, and Curtis was
just too tired to go on. Then he realized where they were; they
were doing the long distance workout for track, and they wouldn't
be done till they'd run up over the butte, across, and all the way
down again. It was just too far for him to go, especially because
he half remembered there was something wrong with his knees.
Then he smiled to himself, and he began to feel sly, because he
remembered the tracks. He looked around, and there they were,
just like they'd been a hundred times before. And he did just what
he always used to do; he waved and said, "See ya, guys," and
took off down the track. He felt smart, only having to go half
as far as anybody else, but he couldn't shake this ghost of a
feeling that it wasn't right to go that way, that something not*

so good would happen if he did and that he'd be sorry, somehow.

And sure enough. He'd lost the tracks now, even though he was still running. Now he was running much harder, and it was on a cinder track, and he understood that he was running the 440, it was the district meet, he had to qualify, and the heat had just started. He was giving it all he had — he felt like he was flying for sure. He was out in front, coming up to the third corner, still leading. Then they were going into the turn, and he could hear running feet coming behind him and everybody yelling at him, all the team and the few people who came to watch, "You're ahead, keep going, keep going! Give it all you've got!" Curtis kept saying to himself, "Go, go, go," but then his feet began to get heavy, or else the track was turning to mud. But he couldn't get his feet to move. His legs just wouldn't move, everyone went running past him, and somebody was just yelling at him, "If you'd just do what you're supposed to! If you just wouldn't take stupid shortcuts! If you'd just think before you do something!" He kept saying, "I'm sorry, I'm so sorry." But it was too bad; he knew he wasn't going to be in the finals, and he began to feel sick again. . .

The darkness in his mind was full of easy, spiralling pictures, pictures of summers gone past, of pipe and more pipe, Jay Stalworthy, his old, crummy truck stuck in the mud, flooded fields, sheep scattering like leaves before the wind, mud. . .and then the old '56 Chevy kind of stabilized his brain. He could see Greg sitting in it with Fillmore, and they were parked at the end of his line. It was very dark because a really angry-looking storm was coming up. He was still moving his pipe, hurrying because the thunder was booming and rolling down around him, and he knew if he didn't hurry, the rain would catch him, and he'd get soaked for sure.

Suddenly the whole place lit up. Curtis saw the bolt of lightning as it hit the Chevy, and he could still hear the air sizzling after it was gone. He ran over to the car. "What's going on?" Greg was asking, looking really surprised. Curtis was afraid to touch the car. He just leaned towards them and said,

*"Man, lightning struck you guys! Did you guys feel that?"
He was thinking that it was a good thing that the tires were
rubber, or those guys would've been fried. Then he thought,
What if lightning had hit the pipe I was moving? I would've
been burnt like a match. What a gross way to go. . . .*

*The pictures began to move again. But this time they were
all scouting, and he began to feel comfortable because he loved
scouting so much; it was so nice to think about. He saw his dad
in uniform, smiling at him, and he saw himself getting his
Eagle. Everybody was talking about how he was the first one to
get his Eagle in the whole ward; then he saw the Tetons.*

*The troop was going to climb the mountain across from
Table Rock. They made a bridge across the river, got to the
mountain, where, using ropes, they began to climb. Finally they
arrived at a rocky part where some huge boulders looked like
they had broken off the mountain, and along the side was a very
sheer cliff with a two hundred foot drop.*

*So they started climbing up the mountain, going through
the cedars, finally reaching timberline where no trees or plants
grew, and the snow was up on top. They finally reached the
top and looked across the Grand Teton, . . . it was beautiful.
He remembered the night before, everybody talking about wild
things like flying saucers and spirit life, and one of the guys
was saying, "I bet you there's a cave over there in that Grand
Teton where the flying saucer spirits go."*

*They were talking about crazy things like that, and they
looked over the mountain range — it was fantastic because
of its beauty. They could almost touch it, and Curtis was saying,
"One day I'm going to climb you." Then he began to feel kind
of sad. And then somebody yelled, "The snow's red," and
everybody had to go see. One of the guys said, "Hey, that
tastes just like watermelon," and they all thought he was making
it up, but he finally got them to try it, and it really did taste
that way. Curtis was explaining to somebody: "There's this
bacteria that gets into the snow and makes it go this way. . . ."*

Then they were jumping off the snow and sliding part

way down a little cliff. It was like wintertime in the middle of summer. The counselor said, "Okay, you guys, we've gotta go." He left Curtis and another scout to make sure everybody came. But they kept straggling behind because Grover had to take pictures of everything. Soon there were a couple of guys down with the counselor, with the rest of the guys hanging back, and Kenny somewhere in the middle.

There was a good snow slide along the side of the mountain, and Kenny got on it. They were all sliding down on their feet. Then Kenny decided to get down on his rear and slide. He was yelling and really moving. As Kenny got about seventy feet away from everybody else, he turned around and waved, went through some trees, and then it was quiet. It was more than just quiet; it was still, like he'd never been there at all. They went running down, trying to find out what happened; they saw that there were only a few trees and then a cliff. Somebody got close enough to the edge to look down, and he could see Kenny, lying very still about a hundred and fifty feet down.

They could see in the snow where he'd turned over on his stomach to grab something. It happened so fast he didn't even have a chance to scream. It can happen that fast. It was weird.

The counselor said to them, "If you guys would only stay together like you're supposed to. If you guys in the rear would have pulled up the tail like you're supposed to, this wouldn't have happened." And Curtis was saying, "I told you I was sorry, what do you want. . . ." And then Curtis felt that he, too, was falling, only slowly, so slowly. . . .

He saw the power pole, and as he began to climb it, it became too much, and he struggled to get away. He was confused and frightened, and he began to feel pain. "I won't climb it," he assured somebody, whoever it was that was hurting him. His senses began to awaken, one by one. . .all painful, all horrible.

He opened his eyes, too wide at first. Even the light hurt, and his stomach heaved. He opened his eyes again and caught a blur of green outside the window; then they gave him another shot, and everything turned around and began to fade again. It came to him, just before he went under, that he must be in an ambulance, and they were going down a residential street. Finally the morphine took him, and he was quiet.

The emergency room staff at LDS Hospital in Salt Lake was prepared; the struggle with death was no new thing to them. The physician who had done the initial exam made the following entry into the medical record:

> Electrical burns of both legs, and complains of painful neck and left flank in addition to severe pain in legs.
>
> Head — normocephalic
>
> Eyes — left pupil dilated and fixed
>
> Neck — the post aspect tender
>
> Has definite point tenderness over the spine
>
> Ears OK. Facial bones — intact
>
> Chest — lungs clear — same tenderness over the left costal margin
>
> Heart — NSR normal
>
> Abdomen — same tenderness in lateral left flank approaching to paraumbicular area. Minimal bowel sounds. Flank appears slightly swollen and bruised
>
> Genitalia — 2nd degree burns of scrotum at junction of thighs

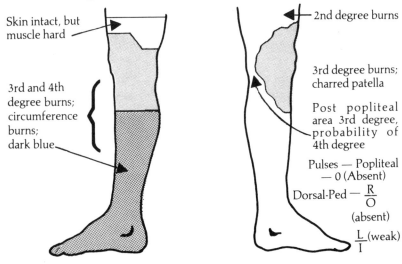

Skin intact, but muscle hard

3rd and 4th degree burns; circumference burns; dark blue

2nd degree burns

3rd degree burns; charred patella

Post popliteal area 3rd degree, probability of 4th degree

Pulses — Popliteal — 0 (Absent)

Dorsal-Ped — $\frac{R}{O}$ (absent)

$\frac{L}{I}$ (weak)

They did what they could for Curtis — new dressings, more drugs — but it was decided that the major effort had to be the patient's. Curtis was put in a private room. He was watched and monitored carefully, but they didn't think he could last the night. That was what they needed to know — whether or not he had it in him to survive.

The next morning he was still alive. At that point, it was almost a miracle. They moved him into intensive care, and the fight began. A real "esprit de corps" was developing in the staff; they rallied around Curtis like he was some kind of losing cause, so they fought alongside him for his life. They began to win.

Curtis' body began to recover its inner order. While his mind stayed quiet under the drugs, his body began to remember how to function. Hour by hour, quiet progress was made, until Curtis' body finally pulled itself away from death, and the medical team allowed themselves to believe the boy would live.

It was toward dusk that first day when Curtis finally approached being fully awake. The physician in charge had decided to cut back on the pain medication, so Curtis came closer to the real world than he had been since he'd left the hospital in Idaho, only to find that this real world was only dull ache in his legs and occasional burning flashes of pain that sliced sharply through what medication there was.

The medical personnel knew they had to keep Curtis going. If they let him slip away mentally, there would have been little they could have done for his body. They talked to him, kept him awake, kept him functioning. If they'd left him alone, he would have faded; he just didn't have it in him to keep his own mind going.

He was lying in intensive care, often nauseated, in pain, and wired to monitors that lit the place up like it was Christmas and summarized his condition with the crazy lines on their little screens. There was an I.V. bottle hanging above his head and the solution it held came down, drip by drip, through a plastic tube and finally through the needle that pierced the back of his hand. The tape over the needle itched.

They had him under a sort of tent. It was a half-hoop affair, designed to keep the blankets off his legs; the kind of burn he had suffered had to be kept isolated.

There he was, wired, taped, tented, in the middle of the intensive care unit while white flurries of nurses were working everywhere to keep death away. Even if they hadn't been giving him something to dull his perception of the pain, the whole thing would have seemed unreal.

Finally, one of the nurses came to Curtis, asking him how he was doing.

"Gross," he replied, and his face told her that and more.

"Time for a little more help, I think," she said and slipped a needle into Curtis' arm. This time they put him out, and while he was sleeping, moved him to a new place, a calmer one that testified of the doctors' faith that he was more or less out of the immediate danger of death.

The first thing Curtis said as he struggled out of that sleep was "My apron caught, my apron caught. . . ," and they knew how important it was that he be kept calm, that he be com- forted. They had the monitors on him, keeping a close eye on his vital signs. Dr. Dingman came in to perform the debridement, or surgical removal of the dead tissue. All that was obviously dead had to be removed. Then everything was redressed and bandaged. It was all that could be done at that point . . . then just waiting.

All through that day Dr. Dingman ordered records of the readings and spinal films. He had to have as much information about Curtis' body as he could get; he realized that if Curtis were to survive, some monumental and far-reaching decisions would have to be made in the next few hours. The doctor was not looking forward to his next talk with Curtis' folks.

It was a hard exchange for all of them. Dr. Dingman sat them down and spoke simply:

"Mr. and Mrs. Brinkman. . . ,"

"Dr. Dingman," Mrs. Brinkman replied, "I want you to know that we are feeling very blessed that our son is *alive*."

The doctor studied her face a moment, understanding that what she had said was an acceptance of whatever he had to tell her. What a horrible thing to happen to these people, he thought. What agony they must have passed through these last two days, watching someone they obviously love so much suffer and not knowing what would come next. He smiled at them a little, trying to convey his sympathy without frightening them but by letting them know they would need it.

"This is Curtis' situation. He has stabilized. We have every reason to believe he has a very good chance to stay alive. But we don't know for certain, and we can't know for awhile yet. We've just got to wait and see what he does. It may take weeks." They nodded with understanding.

"The electrical charge that caused all of this made two exits from Curtis' body, or an entrance and an exit. We can't tell for sure. One exit went down through Curtis' left leg and burned a hole, two inches in diameter, down through the bottom of his foot. The other entrance or exit has come through his groin area. We don't know yet how damaged the digestive tract and pelvic organs are. The other leg is also badly burned." He paused in spite of himself. He wanted this to sound as matter of fact as possible. It was never easy.

"We do know that the left leg should be amputated below the knee. There is too much dead tissue there. If we don't remove it, the leg will become gangrenous. You understand this?"

They nodded again, this time a bit more as if they hadn't heard. . . . "We would like to perform that operation early tomorrow, with your permission. Now, is there anything else I can tell you? Are there questions you need to have me answer?"

They had a few. Nothing of consequence — just something to stall off having to sign the forms, as if something could happen in those few minutes to change things, as if signing the forms made the thing final. At least he's out of intensive care, they thought. They signed the forms and then felt their exhaustion.

They asked if they could see Curtis for a moment; Curtis' dad had to go home. There were other children at home, and he had to work. Dr. Dingman smiled again, a tight little smile. "Just don't wake him," he said, and then he left them.

Curtis was asleep. It wasn't an easy rest, however. The strain of the pain and the trauma showed through the veil of chemical rest, and he looked troubled. It was not easy for either parent to see their son carrying a burden like that, one they couldn't really help him lift. Neither one of them spoke, careful of Curtis' rest, but they looked at each other with strength in the exchange.

They left the room and went out to the parking lot. They spoke of practical matters, allowing the normal business of life to soothe them. They didn't ask aloud, will anything really be normal again? They let the question go, trusting that it would answer itself in time.

"I love you," Raymond Brinkman said to his wife. Then he got in the car and left. She stayed to keep a mother's vigil. It was a funny kind of relief she felt, seeing her husband drive away. "Strange," she said, "but it really is easier to have only one here to worry about." Even so, when he had left, her husband had taken with him a large part of her strength.

Curtis' mother was asleep. They had put a roll-away cot in a little room, not far from Curtis, and there she had gone to rest herself from the bedlam of the last two days. She had been afraid she wouldn't be able to sleep, but her weary body had taken matters into its own hands, and she slept soundly.

At 4:00 a.m. she awoke. Someone was shaking her gently.

"Mrs. Brinkman," the little nurse whispered. "Mrs. Brinkman. You've got to come. Curtis has taken a bad turn, and we've got to take him back down to intensive care. He's developed a high fever. We thought you'd like to be with him while he's moved."

Mrs. Brinkman sat up and found her shoes. This was all so strange. She became frightened as she followed the nurse down the hall. She wondered if he was going to make it or not. It would be so much easier if she just knew. When she saw Curtis' face, she ached for him.

"Mom, this is so bad. This is so bad. When do I start feeling better?"

She smiled at him. "It's all right," she said. "You just have to be patient, Curtis. Just try." She used the same tone of voice with him then as she had always used when he was sick. I'll pretend he's little again, and it's only red measles, she thought. It made things easier. "When do mothers get to break down?" she asked silently, reminding herself that Curtis needed her strength and serenity.

The move was finally complete. Curtis was much more aware at that point than he had been, and any bumping or jerking of the bed, however slight, caused him to scream in pain. Helping Curtis took his mother's mind off her misery; for awhile it made her feel like a mother, all business, all strength. It was funny how action and movement could act as an analgesic.

After Curtis was settled, Dr. Allen took Mrs. Brinkman aside and explained the situation to her.

"Mrs. Brinkman, what we worry about most in burn cases is infection. Now, Curtis has started one; that's why he's got that fever. His body is fighting it. We tried to help by treating it with penicillin, but Curtis had an allergic reaction to it, so we tried another antibiotic which he seems to be accepting just fine. Pretty soon now we'll be taking him into X-ray so we can determine how much of the leg we'll have to remove. You go and try to get some rest. I'll keep you posted, I promise. If you don't hear anything, it's because everything is okay. Okay?" Dr. Allen smiled, and he patted her arm. "Don't worry too much," he said. "We're all pulling for you and Curtis."

Mrs. Brinkman remembered that last part when she was back in her room, alone. "This is when mothers get to fall apart," she said and let herself cry.

The next few hours were full of heavy activity. The surgeons amputated Curtis' left leg below the knee, and they completely debrided the right leg. The nurses fought Curtis' infection, trying to keep enough fluids in him. That evening Dr. Allen went in to Curtis and woke him gently. He had to tell the boy about the operation, what they had done, why they had done it. He did the best he could to make it easy for Curtis, and Curtis seemed to take it very well, although Dr. Allen suspected that he didn't really understand what had happened.

The next morning, July 9th, three days after the accident, Curtis' fever had reached 105, and it would not respond to the cooling therapy. Curtis was in serious condition. He complained of cervical neck pain and headache. The combination of sustained fever and pain that affected the entire central nervous system caused the medical team to suspect a Clostridia infection — a very dangerous situation.

Curtis remained quiet the rest of that day, but even the pressure of a hand on the bedsheets caused him great anguish. He was given several units of blood, but he had an allergic reaction to something in the transfusion, and his torment was multiplied by the development of a severe rash. They were able to treat this quickly, and it seemed to cause no permanent damage.

A routine began to develop, something that Curtis' mother could understand and depend upon through the long hours she was spending by her son's bedside. It was an endless process of dressings, tests, EKS, and constant monitoring of vital signs. But the infection remained and the fever with it. They had to keep Curtis full of morphine, and sometimes he felt like he was floating around the room. His condition was deteriorating, and the situation grew more critical.

The next day was even worse. The infection was so bad that his body was pushing itself to extremes, defending itself against the toxic intrusion. His heart rate reached 140 beats a minute, twice what it should have been. His blood pressure was very high, and the fever raged on. His right leg and what remained of his left were draining toxic wastes, so finally, at 6:30 that morning, emergency surgery was performed. They had to amputate again, this time taking the left knee and what had been left below it.

Curtis received another transfusion, but every time they gave him blood, he got huge hives.

Dr. Dingman was becoming concerned about the right leg. Though there was still evidence of some circulation below the knee, the leg had been shattered by the power of the electricity, and there was no way it would ever again be functional. If things had stabilized at that point and Curtis had healed the way he was, it would have been to live the rest of his life with a quarter of a leg on one side and a whole, but inoperable, leg on the other.

Later that day, when Dr. Dingman changed the dressings on the whole leg, he observed that the ones he removed were green and pungent. He suspected a pseudomonia infection. More debridement of that leg followed. That evening it was noted in the medical record that the remaining leg was "not looking good for ultimate survival."

It was a hard time for Curtis, a bitter time. When he wasn't submerged in morphine, he was in great pain. He couldn't even move his head without hurting. He couldn't tolerate any stimulation at all. He could feel it when anyone walked into his room, and even the thought of the morning bed change was anguish.

This discomfort wasn't limited to his body alone. It is understandable that his mind was also in pretty bad shape. It was a difficult thing, losing a leg, maybe two. Something that was impossible to cope with. The reality was impossible, and the implications of the reality were impossible.

In his anguish, he struck out, mostly at his mother. He was uncooperative and hard to get along with. He complained and wept.

From this point on, he was in the operating room every other day. They never transferred him from bed to table to bed; he never could have handled that much trauma. They moved his entire bed, sparing him as much pain as possible.

Curtis' parents were not given much hope. The staff was frank, and the night of the eleventh was very hard for them. It looked as if the other leg would have to come off. "A week ago,"

Mrs. Brinkman muttered, "I didn't know any of this would happen. Last Thursday I was just wondering if I had enough bread to make lunches for the next week. Last Thursday Curtis was just fine. And now, tomorrow, he may be a double amputee; a sixteen-year-old double amputee. These things just don't happen."

But the next morning there was little question about what would have to be done. The drainage and odor from the remaining leg had increased steadily through the night. It was a question of saving Curtis' life. The decision was made: the right leg had to come off.

Throughout the day the fever raged uncontrollably. The infection deepened. The pain, already terrible in both legs, rose and spread into his abdomen. His scrotum became greatly enlarged, and the physicians feared that other interior organs had been damaged. The bleeding and drainage continued. They had to keep giving him transfusions, but somehow he made it through the night.

Very early the next morning Drs. Broadbent, Dingman, and Stevenson went to work on Curtis. They amputated the remaining right leg, taking it off above the knee. The groin burns were debrided, as were those left on the right stump. Another blood transfusion was given.

He came through. He seemed to be able to tolerate the operation, and by the afternoon, he started taking oral liquids again.

Curtis' mother began to feel some hope. She had been doing her best to support Curtis through all of this, but it had been hard to rise above her own despair. This new hope made things easier.

"Curtis," she said, trying to reach him. "You are going to make it. You'll learn to use artificial legs, and your life will go on. You have to have faith in your Father in heaven, Curtis. He will pull you through this."

"*Through* this," he said, looking up at her. "Mother, you talk as if this was some kind of disease I could get *well* from. Mother, I don't have any *legs*. You can't get well from that."

"But, honey, you're *alive.*"

"Big deal, Mom. What use is being alive? There were so many things I was going to do. Now I can't do *anything.* Everything hurts me so bad, and even if that stops someday, what's the use? I was going to be big, Mom. Now I'm a freak. I'm not Curtis Brinkman anymore; now I'm just some geek on stilts. Mother, make this not be true; oh, Mom, make this just a bad dream I can wake up from."

Curtis was crying. His mother was crying, too. It was all she could do. She couldn't say anymore. What could she say? She had to admit to herself that more than once the last few days she'd had to push pictures out of her mind . . . pictures of those ragged men with no legs, sitting on corners, begging. She'd seen them. What else could a man do with no legs? How could she comfort him? Oh, Heavenly Father, there's got to be a way out of this, her mind cried. You've got to show us. What can I do for him, now — when he's so hopeless, and I'm so scared?

She looked down at her son. She couldn't even touch him for fear she'd increase his pain. She thought again about what she could do.

CHAPTER THREE
Struggle to Survive

The next day was July 14th. It was not an easy day. They kept Curtis under morphine, but the pain cut right through it, and his brain was full of screaming. The pain just wouldn't stop. He couldn't sleep. His mother and father were both there, and he was sharp with them, irritated at the slightest thing.

There was still more draining, and the smell from his wounds was foul. There was a bed change made that nearly drove him wild. For hours afterwards he was upset.

Time passed so slowly. All he could do was lie there, hurting and draining and being angry. It was a long day. In the evening some friends came by. Curtis was reserved and despondant so they left.

Dr. Dingman came in to check his patient. He wasn't pleased with the discharge. He didn't let his worry show, of course, but Curtis knew something wasn't right. Dr. Dingman was sociable enough, but all the time his mind was going over the signs, and his conclusion was flashing red: clostridia, the infection they had feared all along.

There was a parade of doctors after that, all examining, taking vitals, smiling and encouraging. Dr. Dean thought a little clean up would help things along, so he sent a nurse in to size up the situation. She was appalled to realize that, while they had been working like crazy on Curtis' legs, the other end of him had been grossly neglected. His hair still had the original mud in it. It wasn't surprising that no one had tried shampooing it yet. Approaching Curtis with anything less than a life and death matter was like coming up on a lion with a fly swatter.

"What'sa matter," he asked her, his eyes narrowed. He was a very suspicious person these days.

"You're pleasant today," she said.

"What're you looking at?" he asked, not one bit less watchful.

"I think it's your hair," she said, "but I can't tell. It's doing a great impression of a wasp's mudnest. You've been here two weeks, and you're still an incredible mess."

His eyes widened with horror. "You can forget that right now. Lady, you breathe, and it hurts me. You can forget my hair. I'm not kidding." He knew she could do it to him if she decided she should, so he was really pleading.

The nurse was a little perplexed. She knew all about pain, but she also knew what kind of effect clean hair could have on a person's morale . . . and Curtis' morale was a major factor in his healing.

She relented. "Don't sweat it," she said, smiling at him kindly. "We won't do it today, anyway." Then she left, all the time figuring out how she could dry shampoo it while he was anesthetized. It wouldn't be hard; they had to put him out every time they did anything, including change his linen. So that's what happened. She did it while he wasn't looking. The change alone was a relief; beyond that, he found that feeling clean also made him feel human, which made things a lot easier on everybody.

In fact, the effect of the shampooing was so therapeutic Curtis was able to sleep well that night for the first time, and in the morning he ate solid foods for breakfast. This emotional progress was sort of a turning point. Not long after, Dr. Dingman's examination turned up much happier results. He was able to tell Curtis' parents that the infection seemed to have receded a bit, that it might even be ready to clear up.

The news made the Brinkmans feel like they had come out of the woods at last. They were tired. The all night vigils and the constant state of suspense, coupled with Curtis' sharpness, had told on them. This one positive indication gave them something to lean on for awhile and that bolstered up the support they could give their son. That evening the family relaxed and watched T.V. together.

After the nurses had given Curtis an alcohol rub and powdered his back, Dr. Dean came in to change the position of Curtis' stumps. He was a nice man. Curtis needed to talk to someone like that, someone who was nice but who wasn't family.

"Doctor, learning to use artificial legs — is it hard?"

"It takes work, Curtis. You'll have to work at it and not get discouraged."

"Is it weird?"

"You mean, will it feel strange to you?"

"Well, yeah. And will I *feel* weird, you know, being a person with artificial legs?"

"I imagine it will feel weird at first. You know, any new thing takes getting used to. But once you get used to it, I don't think it'll be weird. No. You'll probably forget you have them on at all."

"Really?"

"Yeah."

"What about women?"

"What *about* women?"

"Do I have a chance? Will my legs just make me a freak?"

"Curtis. Your legs are not going to make a significant amount of difference to any girl who's worth having. You hear me? If they don't care about *you* more than they get put off about your legs, they aren't worth it. Okay?"

"I hear you. I just wish I could believe it. That's all. And what about a living? Can a person with no legs make a living? I could work in a store or something, couldn't I? I could do something worthwhile, couldn't I?"

The doctor looked hard into the boy's face. The worries sounded so . . . so young. "And yet," he said to himself, "how would *you* do, Dean, if it happened to you?"

"Curtis," he said, point blank, "you will be able to do anything you have the courage to do. Anything. I mean that. It's up to you. The only thing that will make you a cripple is your own mind." Curtis just looked at him. "And you can begin by accepting the help that people are trying to give you right now. Okay?"

Curtis replied, "We'll see."

That night Curtis slept again. It was progress.

Still in intensive care, Curtis had taken a turn for the better but was continually in tremendous pain and had to come to grips with his mental distress. He asked for medical relief often, sometimes much too often.

The medical staff had to be tough. It was a hard business they were in, watching people suffer, forcing people to do the things that were good for them, even in the face of great anguish. But they were desperate to give Curtis as much relief as possible, and his stay in intensive care was softened by the morphine they gave him.

One afternoon he had just been given a shot. It had relieved him almost immediately, taking the top off his discomfort. He felt light and foggy; he began to float. He was used to floating. It was comfortable.

Then suddenly he began to speed up. It was like his feet were pointed out into space, and he was beginning to fly, really fly. Wild colors and shapes began to fly out at him, whipping by, exploding in his eyes. He screamed.

He yelled, "I'm flying. Somebody get me. Somebody hold me down. . . ."

Dr. Dean rushed in by the bed, holding onto Curtis, saying, "I've got you. I've got you, Curt. You're okay. You're down. We've got you. Relax."

And Curtis was yelling, "Oh, I'm flying. I'm going!" the whole time.

Dr. Dean looked across at the nurse, who looked a little scared. They held him until he came down, staying with him until he could relax enough to fall asleep.

"Too much morphine," Dr. Dean said. "And way too much pain."

A few days later they moved Curtis to a room near the nurses' station. They were not sure of him yet and wanted to keep a close watch even though there was no longer need for intensive care. Improvement began, but misery continued — horrible bedsores were plaguing him and as always, the constant pain, although he was better at coping with it. The sleep was little, but it did come and along with it the ability to consume some solid foods.

Even though the nurses had to put him out before he could be moved, there was better color in Curtis' face. He was bored with television, and he wanted something to *do*. Someone notified the rehabilitation therapy ward that Curtis Brinkman was finally coming around. Curtis' parents were relieved. They could finally do something active to help their son. The danger was gone. At least that's what the room change seemed to be saying.

That afternoon they took a little stroll around the floor, glancing into rooms as they passed, feeling brave enough to have a look at the other burn victims and being happy that Curtis was becoming less and less of a special case every day. They ran into Dr. Dean at the nurses' station.

"Good afternoon, Mr. and Mrs. Brinkman. Did you get a decent rest last night?"

"Yes, we did, finally," Mr. Brinkman told him. "We're feeling so good about the progress Curtis has been making, we can finally relax." Their smiles were easy, and the Dr. could read confidence in them.

"Folks," he said, "I have to be straight with you. I'm glad you're feeling the way you are. Curtis will pick up those kinds of feelings; it will do him a world of good just to be in the same room with the way you're feeling. But I have to warn you . . . I feel like he's got a good shot, a very good shot at making it, but he just isn't out of the woods yet. That infection is still a very real threat. We don't know how extensive the burn damage is in his abdominal area. There are an awfully lot of 'ifs.' "

He was sorry he had to say it. There was such a delicate

balance in situations like this. He could see the struggle these two
people were going through and could see in Mrs. Brinkman's face
that she was regretting the moment of luxury they had been
enjoying. She had known it was too early for expectations like
that. Now the reality seemed even harder. "I'm sorry," Dr. Dean
said. Mrs. Brinkman shook her head, absolving him of any blame,
but there were tears in her eyes.

"Dr. Dean, when will we know?" Mrs. Brinkman asked.
"That's the hard part, not being able to at least settle down and
accept something."

"Well, I think if Curtis can make it for two more weeks, with
everything functioning, we can figure that he's going to live.
Now I want you to understand . . . I've told you these things to
prepare you in case things should go bad on us. I'm not expecting
that they will, but we all have to be prepared in case they do.
Stay positive. Help Curtis to plan his life; keep him as happy and
active as you can. It really does help."

Curtis' father shook the doctor's hand. "You'll always tell us
the truth, won't you, Dr. Dean? The truth. It would be easier to
know for sure than to be deceived, even if it were out of
kindness."

"I promise you that I will. Now listen — there's a lot to be
happy about here. When I examined Curtis that first time, I was
sure he'd never make it through the night. That kid's a fighter
from the word go. He may act like he's given up, and he hates the
whole lot of us for what he's done to himself, but he's gaining all
the time. I don't know, maybe his anger gives him strength. I'll
tell you, if we all do what we need to, Curtis is going to make it."

The Doctor shook Mr. Brinkman's hand. "You're good
folks," he said, and then he left them. When they got back to
Curtis' room, they found him sleeping. A nurse came softly across
the room and led them back out into the hall.

"Curtis has had a little episode of crying out in his sleep. The
pain is probably giving him nightmares. Also, I let him know that
Dr. Dean will be leaving the hospital in September, and Curtis got
really upset. He said he was only staying in this hospital another

two weeks anyway, then he was going home. I wanted you to know. He might say something about it when he wakes up."

Actually, Curtis didn't feel much like talking when he woke up, so everybody settled back and watched T.V., a thing that would happen over and over again in the weeks to come.

The next few days were all the same. Curtis woke at around five, feeling the pain, of course, and feeling a heavy weight on his legs. Sometimes his feet would itch or get very cold, then he would remember all over again that he didn't have feet anymore. He usually woke up soaked with sweat, aching all over. Nurses would come in, giving medication, taking vital signs, bringing bedpans, checking bandages. They had put him on an air mattress now; his bedsores were something frightening. In the morning they'd come in and adjust the mattress.

After all of that, they'd bring him breakfast, or if it were an operation day, pre-op medication. Very often it was an operation day. They still had to anesthetize him before they could take him, even though they moved the entire bed.

By seven, a veritable bevy of physicians had dropped by, checking, asking questions, smiling, passing on. Next came the bed bath and back rub. Then the oral care. All of these things were very painful. But Curtis felt better after they had been done, so he endured. But not without protest; he was still hard to get along with.

The day was endless: back rubs, bed pans, pain, vital signs, T.V., checker games with the folks, afternoon visitors that Curtis couldn't always remember having, mood swings, pain, frustration, medication, constipation, dozing, sudden nightmares, screaming, reading, itching, bedsores, discomfort, catheter and dressing changes — groin and stumps, burning urine, cribbage with the doctors, pain, pain, and pain again. Dr. Dean was the best with Curtis. He could get him to smile.

Curtis' body was working so hard, so hard to recover, but the fight was to go on and on. The infected groin and stump areas still discharged, weeping a yellow-brown, foul smelling liquid.

His temperature still raged, and Curtis was soaked with sweat. Sometimes Curtis dozed, and sometimes he would wake up screaming. Once he dreamed that he'd fallen twenty-five feet into power lines.

The nurses did their best to comfort him. He'd chill, and his legs ached unceasingly. The pain was so constant and so persistent that Curtis was on the verge of tears for hours and hours at a time, finally sobbing aloud. His parents tried so hard to help him, to comfort him, but so often he could not or would not be comforted.

At times he was so miserable he thought death would be a blessing. Curtis watched as the nurses changed his dressings, making the faces that they tried so hard not to make. He knew the wounds had to be kept open, or the infection would spread inwards, and then he really would die. The smell, the sight, and his imagination were almost too much to handle, and he dreamed of having all his wounds permanently bound up so that no one would ever see them again.

Every time the nurses came near him with the dressing wagon, Curtis tensed up. He was growing intensely afraid of the pain involved in changing those dressings. He was always given valium before they started, but it didn't help. The pain got around it.

Curtis had to deal with horrible muscle spasms, cramps that happened in both stumps, which tore screams from him before he knew what was happening. When that happened, it frightened his parents, and they would leap out of their chairs in alarm, only to stand helplessly by, afraid of touching their son and increasing his pain.

There was operation after operation. Some were routine, removing necrotic and dying tissue. Some were frightening, especially when Curtis hemorrhaged — stemming the flow of blood was a horrible fight. Over a period of days, they had to pump thirty-two units of blood into Curtis, replacing what he was losing from his stumps and his abdominal area. Every time they gave him blood he developed horrible hives.

It was telling on Curtis, destroying his emotional control, dissolving his mild temper. He knew that he loved his parents, but he was constantly striking out at them verbally. They were the close ones, the ones he knew, the ones he was most comfortable with, so they bore the brunt of his distress. It was hard on them, but they struggled to hold on to their patience, refusing to be hurt by their son's apparent hatred. They knew they could only guess at what he was going through.

Nothing was easy. First Curtis would go through terrible constipation. Then it was diarrhea. He would just get through that when his stomach would begin aching. Also, there was the horrible nausea, or the bedsores on his back and buttocks itched and ran, tormenting him. All in all it was pure agony.

There were periods when Curtis vomitted continually. When that happened, they would stick him full of tubes and keep an I.V. going so he wouldn't dehydrate. Once he felt a warm, runny, salty fuzziness in his throat; he began to spit up bright blood, all the while bleeding from both nostrils. Dr. Dingman was called immediately. He came right in and packed both nostrils, at last controlling the bleeding. There were more tubes, this time in his nostrils, and there was medication with another I.V. It was a hard night. The tubes drove Curtis crazy, and he yanked the packs out, causing the bleeding to start again. Then the same procedure had to be initiated again.

There was a headache pounding in his head, and he was so thirsty his mind thought constantly of liquids. He never seemed to get enough. His mouth was always dry, like it was lined with felt. The only relief he got was when they came in to do his teeth. They would rinse his mouth out and that helped a little. He dreamed of tall, iced glasses of 7-up and of frosty, heady mugs of root beer. The dreams only made it worse.

The vomiting got worse and continued until the last week of July. Then, on Friday, Curtis suddenly realized that there was no more nausea. It had quit. Just like that. It would have been a nice thing if Curtis could have shaken the feeling that something was very wrong. He listened to his body, and he began to think that his stomach had died. It was like his entire gastrointestinal system had just shut right down. He began to get scared.

He called for the doctor. His hands were shaking. "I wonder if this is it?" he thought. He reached for the T.V. remote control, not wanting to listen to himself thinking things like that. He could stand about three minutes of Lucille Ball, cracking the audience up, then he turned the thing off, wondering, "How can they be so happy when the world is so gross?"

Finally the doctor came. He listened and prodded and asked questions and finally came to the conclusion that Curtis had been right; the GI tract had quit on them. No one could figure out why it had happened; they had even less idea how they could get things going again. Dr. Dingman tried to make light of the whole thing, but Curtis had too much experience now, reading the truth in people's faces; he knew he was in trouble.

Saturday came, and things were not better. They scheduled him into surgery. It was almost too much for Curtis' parents. They couldn't help remembering what Dr. Dean had said. . .if everything keeps functioning like it should. . . .

Curtis was now entirely dependent on the glucose in his I.V. Dr. Dingman told Curtis' folks that he needed to do exploratory surgery.

"Is he in good enough shape for that kind of thing?" Mrs. Brinkman asked. She didn't need to ask. She was just hoping someone would tell her things weren't as bad as they were.

"Mrs. Brinkman," the doctor said, "it's going to be touchy. Abdominal surgery is risky at best, and Curtis' body has had about all anyone can take. But, ma'am, if we don't get things going again, he has no chance at all. We just have to do the best we can. We're going to wait until Monday. If nothing new develops by then, we'll have to do what we can."

Later, after the doctor left, Mr. Brinkman turned to his wife. "Karma. We need to give the boy a blessing. The doctor is a good man, and I'm learning to love him, but he is just as lost about this as we are. This is when we need the Lord most. I'm going to call Brother Brown to assist me. You tell Curtis. Everything will be fine."

It echoed in Mrs. Brinkman's mind, the confidence and faith she had just heard. Her heart told her he was right. She gave her worry to her God.

Mr. Brown walked quickly from the elevator to room 611. The phone call he'd just received had caused him to leave his Saturday afternoon gardening immediately. He had cleaned up and put on his dark blue suit and had gotten to the hospital as quickly as he could. It was a solemn and holy thing, being asked by a father to help administer to his son.

The initial pleasantries over, there was a pause, common to all such events, in which everyone composed their spirits, readying themselves for the tremendous business at hand. There was a strong, quiet spirit in the room as Brother Brown annointed Curtis' head with the oil. He carefully allowed a tiny drop of the consecrated oil to darken Curtis' hair. Then he set the tiny vial down on the white metal table beside him and placed his two hands on Curtis' head over the oil. Everyone closed their eyes.

"Raymond Curtis Brinkman. In the name of Jesus Christ and by the power of the Melchizedek Priesthood, I annoint you with this oil, which has been consecrated, dedicated, and set apart for the healing of the sick in the household of faith, and I do so in the name of Jesus Christ. Amen."

Brother Brown moved aside, making room for Curtis' father to join him, he, also, laying his hands on the boy's head. They were quiet for a few moments, seeking the spirit of the Lord. Then Mr. Brinkman spoke with power and emotion:

"Raymond Curtis Brinkman. In the name of Jesus Christ and by the power of the Melchizedek Priesthood, we lay our hands upon your head and seal this annointing whereunto you have been annointed by one having authority. . . ." He went on, blessing Curtis' body that it would rally to fight the infection, that his digestive tract would resume its normal function, and that Curtis would be raised from his bed of affliction to experience once again vigorous health.

Curtis was reminded that he was a son of God, that great

blessings were in store for him if he would remain close to the gospel of Jesus Christ. Then Mr. Brinkman asked the Lord to bless the doctors and nurses and any other person involved, that their actions and decisions in relation to Curtis would be wise and correct. He asked a blessing for himself and his wife, and for other family and friends, that they all could be sensitive to Curtis' needs and that their decisions, also, could be wise.

The blessing was closed in the name of the Savior.

Mr. Brinkman embraced his son. Everyone in the room cried. It is hard not to cry in the present of the spirit of the Lord.

By Sunday afternoon, there hadn't been even a hint of activity from Curtis' stomach. They still couldn't feed him, not even a glass of water. He burned with thirst. All of those clichés about being thirsty passed through Curtis' brain at one point or another, and not one of them approached the true condition of his mouth and throat. He was beginning to appreciate the meaning of the word "parched," and he saw his throat in his mind like a mud flat turned into a desert: thick, cracked, flaking.

He could think of nothing but icy water. Curtis pleaded with them, with *anyone*, "Just a little drink, just a very little drink." They couldn't let him have anything. He was going nuts. Finally they figured some ice chips wouldn't hurt, so they brought him some, and he was allowed one tiny chip every so often.

They kept that cup of ice on the table next to the bed. It just sat there, in reach, all the time melting, melting into water.

"Please, Mom, please," he said. His lips were so dry. They cracked when he talked.

"Curtis, you *know* we can't give you anything until you can digest it." She moistened his lips with a rag and then gently rubbed petroleum jelly on them.

Any relief was nice, but nothing was enough.

He lay there, trying to think of something besides his throat and 7-up. He thought about basketball, of all things. He could see himself, tall — almost seven feet — moving up and down the court like lightning. Nothing could touch him. He could feel the sweat running down his throat, wet and salty.

He came to himself, trying to swallow. And he looked down at the bed. "You better stop dreaming that way, Brinkman," he said to himself. "There's nothing under those blankets but gross, sick, ugly stumps. The rest of your life you're gonna be a short person who can't even eat or drink. Not even if you could reach it."

Anger surged up inside of him suddenly, and he wanted to throw something. "If I can't get something to drink in one second, I'm gonna go screaming out of here, and I'm going to throw this bed and everything else out of this window, and I'm going to drag the rest of this stuff with me down the hall when I go." The picture he had in his mind of all those things going on made him feel so satisfied; he was really in the mood to do something reckless.

There were two nurses in the room, his mom, and that glass of melting ice that was about half water by now. No way would they let him get hold of that. Not if they were around. So what was the solution?

"Hey," he said, sounding as put out as he could. "Could you guys please leave so I could go to the bathroom?"

The nurses left. They were used to accommodating people that way. But Curtis' mom had a feeling. . . . She left, but she didn't go far. As soon as the coast was clear, Curtis went after the cup. It was a big problem because the cup was on the same side as the I.V. and maneuvering his body around the needle in his arm was a lot of work. But he did it.

Just as he got the cup in front of him, halfway to his mouth with all that beautiful melted ice, his mother popped back in to check and see if her hunch was right. She made a noise of alarm, leaped for the bed, and grabbed hold of the cup. They fought over it, spilling ice back and forth over the bed, over the floor, everywhere. Curtis began hollering, he was so mad. Mrs. Brinkman couldn't help but see herself there, in the hospital, beating on a howling invalid, but what else could she do?

Finally she won. It made her feel bad, knowing how miserable Curtis was, but she was getting tough. He was going to make it, even if she had to break his arm to keep him alive.

It seemed as if only a short time had passed when a slight sound was heard. It was only a little gurgle, so quiet that at first no one paid any attention to it. Then it suddenly struck Curtis that it had sounded awfully close to home. "Hey, was that me?" he said. Suddenly, everybody came alive.

Curtis didn't even notice how odd it was to have a whole room full of people leaning over him, listening to his abdomen. There was another noise. They sent for the doctor.

When Dr. Dingman got there, he confirmed everyone's hopes. "The machinery is winding up, Curtis," he said. "You're working again. The surgery won't be necessary."

It was like heaven to the Brinkmans. Suddenly, Curtis was going to be all right. None of the doctors could explain why things had stopped in the first place, nor could they explain why it had started again. But Curtis knew what had made him well, and his parents knew. They knew there were problems ahead, but they would be able to sleep at night, now, knowing that things were in the proper hands. Their son was going to live.

Now, it seemed to everyone involved that from this point on things should only get better, but it was not to be. Things were brighter for awhile; the victory of the digestive tract had a great effect on Curtis' morale. But he was still in pain, and what physical progress had begun was tiny and quiet. It didn't take long for Curtis to become discouraged once more.

CHAPTER FOUR
Sweet Success

The nurses did everything they could to make things easier on Curtis. They did simple little things to relieve the pains that made his life so miserable, like putting hot water bottles on his arm when the I.V. was changed or putting ice packs on his head to minimize the constant throbbing there. They took care of his mouth for him and gave him as much pain medication as was allowed.

Even so, Curtis was hard to get along with. He seemed continually exhausted. He was uncooperative, slow to answer questions. He was chronic in his complaints about the pain, asking for medication often, too often, the doctors noted. Once he was given something, he would deny that it had helped him at all, but the nurses could see the relief in his face. He refused solid foods, afraid of more constipation, and his mother had to work with him like she would work with a little child, trying to get him to take anything at all.

There was little conversation in the room, usually only between the nurses and Mrs. Brinkman. Curtis still screamed occasionally when the spasms in his stumps hurt in spite of his medication. There were more operations, more nausea, still more chills.

When the Brinkmans began to feel their faith slip, they would remember the positive things, the kindnesses that had been rendered them. They thought about the Kings whose son had been operated on the day Curtis had first been brought into the hospital. They had offered the Brinkman's their extra car and a place to stay whenever they needed it. There was a nephew in

Salt Lake who also had opened his home to them. Friends from Idaho and Utah sent cards and visited; their LDS bishop from Shelley had driven all the way down to Salt Lake to make sure that they were accepting the situation well. Curtis' irrigation buddies, Tony and Jeff, wrote faithfully.

The people back home had really pulled together, setting aside special days so they could fast and pray together for the family. They gave blood, sent cards, even put on a talent show to raise money for Curtis. It was one of the good things that would come from all of this; that kind of Christlike outpouring would never be forgotten. The love that was coming from outside sustained Curtis' parents when they had little else to rely on.

A man from the LDS Social Services had come to them, helping them understand Curtis and his behavior. He told them that Curtis might withdraw, become introverted. There was the possibility also that he might just do the opposite and become outgoing, overcoming his handicap. He said only time would tell.

No matter what they did, though, things got discouraging. They hoped with all their hearts that Curtis wouldn't turn into a whining, demanding invalid. They wanted him to be happy, productive, to be as normal as he could possibly be. And they hoped he could someday be a father — that was a question still unanswered.

There was a night nurse they loved. When she found out that she would be gone for six days, she fixed Curtis a box of treats with one item he could unwrap each day.

There was another good thing that began to happen; before the accident, Curtis had never been very physical in his expressions of love. Now, even though he was ornery and impossible to deal with — sometimes very unkind — he was hugging his mother, kissing her, and begging her not to leave him. It was enough to make up for the bad times.

One evening, after a particularly bad day, Mrs. Brinkman sat near Curtis' bed, silently soothing herself. She considered her faith. It was so easy to be religious, to talk religion, even to live its precepts. But to understand is another thing. All her life she had been able to speak intelligently about God and the pain He must have suffered, watching the agony of his Son. But now she was beginning to understand it. "Lord, help me do this right," she prayed.

But then she hadn't been doing too badly. One day when Curtis had been having a hard time, she'd encouraged him to talk about it. He'd cried and said, "I really wanted to be tall."

She'd wanted to say the right thing, to meet the problem realistically, but to give him hope at the same time. At the moment, however, she didn't have the time to think out a good, therapeutic answer. All she could do was say the first thing that came to her and that was, "Well, Curtis, it's not all over. Someday you'll get married, and your son will be tall. I mean, it's very likely he'll be a lot like you."

Curtis had looked at her then, the new idea pleasing him. He even smiled. "Maybe so," he said, "maybe so." And it sounded like he was going to be patient enough to find out.

So she had comforted her son. But she had reminded herself of some of her private worries. What girl would want Curtis now? Being married — it was hard enough to find someone under normal conditions. And if he should be blessed enough to find a young girl with that much depth of character, could he have children? Not likely. Judging from the exterior burns, his interior organs were probably gone.

She usually did a very good job of keeping those thoughts at bay. But sometimes, sometimes. . . .

When Curtis looked at the calendar and saw that it was August fifth, it was hard for him to believe he'd been in a hospital for a month. Then as he shifted in the bed, his bedsores screaming at him, he couldn't believe that *only* a month had gone by. He asked one of the nurses for some more pain medication; that was about the extent of his conversation these days. The nurse told him, "No, that it was still way too early," and that finished the ritual.

He lay there after that for what could have been minutes or hours, with nothing to do but watch T.V. or study the pain that seemed to grow in his groin and stomach with every long minute that dragged by. Finally, someone came in to prep him for another operation, and they gave him his pre-op medication. That was nice. Everything began to fade into a pleasant haze, like he was moving away from everything, ever so slowly into the fog. . . .

Then he could hear noises, far away, talking. He tried to focus on the sound, to understand the words. It was like swimming up towards the surface of the water with his eyes open; the water was so heavy. Then there were faces there, growing clearer. Hold still, he thought at them, or maybe he said it, who could tell? The faces were at once strange to him and familiar.

Okay, okay. I'm getting it, he thought. It's the guys from Shelley; it's just the guys from old Shelley.

"How you doin', Curtis?" they said, still sounding very far off, like they weren't really moving their mouths right.

"Just fine, just fine. And how are you guys?" he said back to them as clearly as he could. At least he was sure that was what he'd said. But he saw them kind of looking around and heard someone saying, "What did he say?"

They held something up. "Look Curtis," one of the boys said, a little more clearly. "We brought this for you because we thought maybe you could use something to do, you know? We really want you to have it. It's from all of us. We even made you some tapes to play on it."

They handed it to him to touch. They couldn't really let go of it because he would have dropped it for sure. He kept trying to focus on it; then it came clear. It was a cassette recorder with a radio. It was beautiful.

"Hey, you guys. This is beautiful," he said. "Thank you, thank you." He saw them looking around again, and someone else said, "What did he say?" It was too much work, communicating like this. Everything faded again, like the water was just too heavy, and he sank down into it until everything was just nice and gray and warm, and he was asleep.

Jeff looked at Mrs. Brinkman. "I guess maybe we chose not so good a time, huh?"

"No, boys," she said. "There's hardly a time that *is* good these days. You did just fine, and I know he's going to love having this. It gets so dull for him, lying there."

They all looked down at Curtis, just in case he should still be in there somewhere, but he was gone. So the boys visited with Curtis' folks until they ran out of conversation, then they left. It was kind of unsatisfying, coming all that way just to say "Hi," as though you were shouting down a well, but they felt very good about doing something they knew was nice for Curtis. They left feeling like they had improved his life — and as though they were beginning to make it up to him for letting him climb that pole in the first place.

Curtis was finally moved onto some kind of magic bed that was supposed to give him relief from his bedsores. The nice thing was it actually worked. After the move, he felt good enough to start working out with light weights. The dumbbells he used were only about a pound and a half apiece, but they were still a horrible drain on his strength. It was quite awful, having to face up to the fact that he was so weak. But the exercising seemed to help things, and he began to feel more like eating solid foods.

At this point, the doctors were doing skin grafts on Curtis' stumps, and they were taking skin from healthy parts of his body for the grafts. If that weren't bad enough, the nurses started turning him over on his stomach to take the pressure off his bedsores, and that was horrible. The pain and discomfort he suffered when they turned him over was tremendous, and he spent most of the time crying and begging them to turn him on his back.

Through the first part of August, Curtis' condition remained pretty much the same. Emotionally, he was a mass of contradiction; one minute he was up, the next he was plunged into despair. The grafts began to take, but the donor sights were swollen and painful. They were turning him every two hours now, and it seemed to Curtis that Hell must be just like this, getting over old hurts, then getting new ones before you ever could relax.

His mother started going home during the week. It was nice for Curtis to know that he was well enough so she could feel good about leaving, but it was bad to be alone. When she came back on the weekends, she always brought some of the family with her. Sometimes Greg would come, but when he did, he was pretty quiet. It was hard for Greg. Curtis' accident had affected him more deeply than anyone had realized.

When the family had left again, Curtis didn't feel like he could hold up bravely in front of the nurses, so he started voicing his indignities. He was miserable and made everyone else miserable, too. That was one thing that really worried the staff — Curtis' attitude — the fact that he wasn't learning to cope with the situation.

On August 19, Peg Marshall, a psychiatric nurse who had been working with Curtis, came into his room, smiling, but there was an air of determination about her which made Curtis expect the worst.

"How are you today, Curtis?" she asked, then raised her hand, stopping his answer. "I know," she said. "You don't have to say a thing. Now, Curtis, we've got a little problem here. Dr. Dean asked me to talk to you about it."

Curtis rolled his eyes, thinking it was going to be a good one this time.

"Let's look at your stomach, okay, Kiddo?"

"No one leaves me any dignity around here," Curtis mumbled, but he began, slowly, to pull the sheet back, gingerly moving the gown so that the nurse could see his stomach. What she saw was a scabbed-over donor sight, angry and raw at the edges where the scabs had been picked away.

"Okay, now, Curtis. Look what a mess you're making of that site. Every time you pick at that place you increase the danger of infection, and you make more scar tissue. Now, why are you doing this? Are you bored or what?"

Curtis frowned. He wasn't being perverse, he was just searching around for an answer to her questions.

"Peg, you're not going to believe me, but I didn't even really know I was doing it. I don't know. Maybe it itches, and I just like scratching or something. I don't know. I always used to do that when I was little. Didn't you?"

So Peg sat down with Curtis and talked the problem over, finally coming up with a plan that would help him control his behavior. And that really was the basic idea behind the talk — control. She was teaching Curtis that he needed to take an active part in his healing, that he had options, if only he would exercise them. She then spoke to him about the future, encouraging him, letting him know there were plenty of good things ahead. But all Curtis could see was an operation for every day of his life, operations, bedpans, pain, vomiting, and nightmares. When Peg finally left, it was not with the feeling that she had accomplished anything.

They gave Curtis a trapeze so he could lift himself when he wanted to. They did everything they could to make things nice for Curtis. But he was pulling further and further away, losing his grip on emotional stability. There were long periods of time when he wouldn't communicate at all except when he absolutely had to. The medical staff was worried. Curtis' parents were nearly beside themselves trying to think of something — anything — to help him. Then a major change took place in Curtis' life, a change wrought by the entire congregation of medical people and parents who were desperate to keep him human.

Early on the morning of August 21, the day shift nurse swung into Curtis' room, pulling back the curtains, and flourishing them as the sweet sunlight came cascading through the window.

"Good *morning*," she said, as if someone had cooked her eggs just right at breakfast. "How did you sleep?"

"How am I *supposed* to sleep?" he said, glaring at her.

"That's the joy of my life," she said, beaming at him. She was feeling wonderful, knowing that she knew something he didn't. "Having a patient who is so *grateful* to be alive."

Curtis groaned and put his pillow over his head. "Go away," he said. "You're bothering me." He felt her fiddling around down at the foot of the bed, wondering all the while what that crazy nurse was doing.

Since she gave no explanation and he couldn't see much with the pillow over his face, he took it off so he *could* see, and there, at the end of his bed, were all of his earthly possessions in a nice, big pile.

"Okay, what are you doing?" he asked her.

"If I told you, there'd be no surprise to it at all, now would there?"

"Okay, okay. If that's the way you like getting your kicks, tormenting sick people, fine. I hope you're happy about it."

Just then a couple of green-gowned orderlies came in. The one with the big mustache said, "Okay, Curtis, ready to roll? No pun intended." Everybody but Curtis thought that was pretty funny. The orderlies began to move the bed towards the door. They were still laughing, so they weren't being as careful as they might have been. The look on Curtis' face when they started bumping him around sobered them a little, just enough so that they were at least a bit more careful.

They headed off down the hall, got on the elevator, got off at the sixth floor, and rolled on down to room 611. Curtis had his eyes closed the whole way, and no one would have blamed him if they'd known how easily his stomach could turn itself inside out. They got the bed through the door and scooted it around against the wall, and that was it.

"Well, there you are. A new home," said the nurse who thought she was so funny. "Hope you enjoy yourself. Spread a little of that sunshine of yours around to your new roomies." She patted him on the arm, and he opened his eyes. The room seemed huge after the one he was used to. The nurse was putting away his things; over her back he could see more beds, and when she finally got out of the way, he saw the other guys. There were three of them, two of them giving him the once over, the other seemingly asleep.

"Well, . . . hi," Curtis said. He was kind of embarrassed.

The nurse watched them from the doorway. She was thinking, there now, just try being a self-pitying, big baby when you finally know there are people in the world just as bad off as you are. This'll be good for you, Curtis Brinkman. It didn't take long before the boys were talking and laughing like old friends, and Curtis was doing more interacting in those few minutes than he had for weeks in his old room. It was going to work out just fine. The nurse left, humming.

One of the new guys, Clark, was from Blackfoot, Idaho, a town that was only eighteen miles from Shelley. He had fallen off a hay wagon and broken his back. Next to Clark was Claude. Claude was in complete traction; he was paralyzed from the neck down, the result of a car accident. Bruce was the one who looked like he was sleeping. The other boys told Curtis that Bruce had been in a tragic accident, and that he was in a coma. Curtis finally began to feel like he wasn't alone, that someone else understood how awful it was to have your life so messed up.

The plan couldn't help but work. Who wouldn't have been crazy, shut up for two months with no one but medical people and worried family around, big reminders that something was wrong. Together, the boys talked, remembering the good times, bragging about all the awful things they had done, absolutely cracking each other up over nothing at all.

They called themselves 'The Nudist Colony" because they were all totally naked under their sheets. They made up games, jokes, and gave the nurses fits. In short, they were therapy for each other.

One of their favorite visitors was Dee Dee, the physical therapist. Dee Dee was cute like Connie Stevens: pert, shapely, and feminine. With her, they were shameless. Clark would get her to come over by his bed, then he'd drop something or need to tell her something in a very weak voice, so she had to bend over to hear it. Meanwhile, Curtis would get a nice, long look at her "curvy calves." Then Curtis would need to tell her something. It was really no big thing, but it was sneaky, and it was masculine, so it made them feel alive.

The move had actually been Dr. Allen's idea. He had said, "Curtis is a depressed kid. What he needs is to be with someone who shares his situation. Let's put him in a ward." It was the best thing that could have happened, and Curtis' progress was wonderful. Instead of being so testy all the time, Curtis began to flirt with the nurses, like the other boys did. He finally began looking at them instead of fighting, deciding that he liked what he was seeing. Rosalind and Jane were right up there on the top ten, maybe because they smuggled hamburgers and shakes in every so often.

The emotional improvement began to show up in Curtis' physical behavior. It was getting easier to sit up and move around, with the whirlpool bath finally beginning to feel good. Curtis began to accept his body the way it was, even to the point of getting so he could look down at the stumps of his legs and not be afraid to admit to himself that they were his.

One morning, a tall, rugged looking kid named Mike came in to visit Claude. Actually, Mike was in the hospital because they were going to operate on his harelip. He told Curtis that he'd been playing basketball for the University of Utah and was going pro in the fall. Curtis congratulated him, but all the time, he was thinking to himself, sure you will. You dummy, you'll never make it. You're a dreamer, just like I was. I thought I'd play pro ball, too. It'll never happen.

Curtis was still having his bad moments. And some of his days were very bad. Sometimes the pain, bedsores, and draining of his stumps still got to him, but those times were far fewer, and the days began to fly by.

Mrs. Brinkman had started teaching school again, so she could come to Salt Lake only on weekends. One day she walked into the ward, and there were three lively, healthy-faced boys belching out "Row, row, row your boat" at the top of their lungs. Though totally out of tune, totally non-musical, it was the happiest song she'd ever heard. She was closer to breaking down in front of her son at that moment than she had been through the whole ordeal.

"Hi, Mom," Curtis shouted, waving wildly from the "boat" he was paddling. "Ahoy, there! How is everything?"

"Fine, Curtis," she said. "Just fine."

Life was getting so much better. Curtis was happy these days. He talked just like a normal, healthy person, and there was laughter from his lips. He could sit up straighter and for longer periods of time. Also, there were more visitors, which he handled very well. Curtis didn't know it, but the pain shots he had been depending so much on were slowly being replaced by placebos; he thought he was getting medication, but it was his mind that was beginning to handle the pain. The doctor was taking him off the morphine without any problems. The skin grafts were still taking well. When he got a haircut, it did wonders for his morale. Things were going just fine.

Next, they introduced him to the wheelchair. It began with a slanting one. They laid him down in it, then gradually cranked it up. What a setback! "Here we go again," he mumbled. "If it's not one thing. . . ." Perhaps the worst part about it was that any kind of upright movement made him intolerably dizzy after he'd been prone for months. And close on the heels of dizziness was his old enemy, nausea. That, coupled with the new pains that came with sitting up, made the wheelchair a torture.

The boys encouraged him the best they could.

"Come on, Spud," they shouted at him. "You can do it. Show those nurses what a man you are."

Finally Dr. Allen tried a little motivational psychology.

"You learn to handle that wheelchair," he said, "and you can go to church."

Church had never been that big a treat for Curtis. He'd liked it about as much as any sixteen year old boy likes to sit still. But now the prospect of getting out of the room to function in a normal atmosphere — to get away from himself for awhile — was like some kind of sweet dream. He worked. And on

September sixth, they felt he had worked hard enough.

He couldn't really go in the wheelchair. It would be awhile yet before he had enough skill or strength to endure the chair for any length of time. They just took him in his bed. His mother helped him to dress, and his roommates were as excited as he was about the whole thing.

Actually, it was good to have their support, because getting dressed was painful, and it was very strange to him, having those clothes touching his body after he'd been without them for so long. But everyone else was so happy about him going he decided he was happy, too. As they pushed the bed out the door, he waved at the others and said, "See you after church."

The services were held downstairs for a good-sized congregation of patients and visitors. It wasn't exactly a normal ward with deacons passing the sacrament and babies crying, but it was church, and it was familiar, even fulfilling.

When they finally wheeled him back into his room, he was exhausted. The other boys waited for a decent interval while the shot Curtis had been given took effect. Then they started hitting him with questions: "What was it like? Were there any girls? Were there any *foxy* girls? Did any of them *smile* at Curtis? Did he get to smell any perfume?"

Curtis smiled at them and began to drift away. It had been good, getting out of there. It had been a little step closer toward real life. Right then, he was too close to sleeping to realize how soon he'd have to face the real world, so he wasn't worried about that right now.

That evening, after an afternoon full of family and friends, Curtis had time to think about going back home. It had been nice to have so many visitors. It had been nice to have people around. They all seemed to care about him. Nobody had made him feel strange; in fact, not once had he felt like anything but just Curtis Brinkman. So maybe it wouldn't be so hard.

The more he thought about it, the more he wanted to go home and get things started. He remembered how he'd felt in the beginning of all this, the way he'd felt when people had told him he should be grateful to be alive. He hadn't been grateful, then, but he was now.

He still wasn't sure what was going to happen to him, what his life would be like, but he was glad to have a chance at whatever was going to come. He put the seeds of his fear away, and he began to feel a strange kind of determination. He would make life be good. He would *be* something, even with no legs.

He thought about church that day. They'd all talked about the Lord, how He cared, how He could help. Curtis suddenly came to the point in his life where he had to decide once and for all if he really believed in those things — *really* believed.

He closed his eyes and mentally fell to his knees. He wrestled with his feelings, begging to know, begging for faith, for a testimony of the kind of love he wanted to believe in. He found himself listing blessings and thinking of the ones who had cared for him so carefully through his crisis. He began to love. It welled up inside him and burst into gratitude of the highest order. When he opened his eyes, *he knew.*

And he knew he would make it.

Just before he drifted off to sleep, he said to himself quietly, "I'm going to have a chance to give someone courage, some-day. . . ."

Throughout the next few days, Curtis made great progress. He was getting to the point where he could get himself out of the bed and into the wheelchair. He had more mobility and a new sense of freedom. Teachers came into the ward and conducted classes for the boys. Curtis wanted to go home. He felt ready. He worked like crazy, trying to show the medical staff he didn't need them anymore, and when they didn't run right out and release him, he went on a hunger strike. That didn't last too long, though; he was too healthy to like being that hungry.

Then suddenly, something went wrong. He had been healing up like a dream, and now his right stump began draining again. The pain grew until it was intolerable. He couldn't sit in the chair; he couldn't do anything. The doctors were bewildered.

They kept the whirlpool baths going, and they explored the
stump with great, huge needles. Curtis hated screaming again, but
he couldn't help it when they probed that way.

"What are they *doing* to you?" Clark asked.

"They're killing me," Curtis replied in a painful tone.

"They must be the way you sound."

That helped a little.

Curtis' appetite dropped off, and nothing seemed to be
getting better. Finally, someone thought maybe it was because
Curtis was so anxious about going home. They were willing to
try anything at that point, so the doctors ordered his release,
hoping the resulting emotional relief would heal his body as well.

On Saturday, September 18, the Brinkman family was sitting
around the breakfast table, having pancakes when the phone
rang. Curtis' mom answered.

"Mrs. Brinkman? This is Dr. Allen at Salt Lake. Would you
all like to come get your son today?"

Pandemonium broke loose.

CHAPTER FIVE
The Homecoming

September in Idaho is beautiful. That Saturday afternoon the warm September sun warmed the backs of a bunch of rowdy Shelley teenagers, all congregated in front of the Brinkman place. They were painting huge letters on a long piece of butcher paper, and they were making a real mess of it.

Tony and Jeff stood back, eyeing the thing. As brothers, they didn't always agree, but at that moment, when they looked at each other, it was with a common pleasure.

"Will Greg like it?" Tony asked. "Did we do it like he wanted?"

"Who cares as long as Curtis can read it," Jeff replied, squinting at the second hump in the 'm' on 'home.' "Okay, you guys," he shouted. "Let's shut up and get this thing hung. They would be home any minute. Get up on the garage, Tony."

When they got it up, they figured anybody could read the "WELCOME HOME, CURTIS" from about six blocks away, even if they were blind — which Curtis wasn't — the flourescent paint was so bright. The sign made them feel good. They just wanted Curtis to know how welcome he was.

There still was some time, so they practiced some songs they were going to do when the Brinkmans drove up. These were good old songs, but no one on earth would have recognized the words. They even made up some new verses right there while they were waiting, knocking themselves out being so funny. They kept it up for awhile, all the time keeping an eye peeled for the car. But an hour went by, and still no Curtis. It got to be dinnertime, so people began to wander off toward home. When it got dark, there wasn't a soul left, but the big sign still shouted out its message of love and reassurance.

It had been a long ride for Curtis, and he was beginning to wonder if maybe he'd come home too early, his right stump felt so bad. When they passed the "Welcome to Idaho" sign with the big russet potato on it, he began to feel better. He felt like he'd been gone for years.

When they finally drove through Shelley, the sky was just as dark as it could before night actually fell, and there were very few people on the street. No one seemed to notice them as the Brinkmans drove down the familiar streets, and a little stab of despair cut Curtis' heart.

This is about the most important moment of my whole life, coming home, and I feel like nobody even cares that I'm finally back. He was thinking other dismal things of that order when they turned down their own street. The sight of such familiar things was enough to make the tears come into Curtis' eyes, and when they pulled into the driveway, there was the big sign, flapping a little in the September evening draft. The tears spilled right over onto his face.

"Welcome home," his mother read aloud. She didn't say anything else. She didn't need to.

Curtis had a long time to plan what his first week home would be like. He'd thought he was prepared for just about any contingency, the triumphant and the horrible, but being in bed for a week, sick and exhausted, had never entered his head as a possibility.

It was downright discouraging, not to say anticlimatic. There were so many people he wanted to see, and so many that wanted to see him, but he was so weak, so tired all the time, he just couldn't handle the strain of socializing. Anyway, he was still taking some medication because his right stump was killing him all the time, so he spent a lot of time doped up, not exactly the best condition for coherent conversation.

Curtis' mom was worried. She had wanted it to be all over,

all the worry and fear, so they could start working on putting Curtis' life back together, but here they were back again, not knowing what was wrong or what would come of it.

There were a few visitors who made it into Curtis' room that week, old friends — good friends. And it was so nice to hear about what was happening at school — who was going together, how the football team looked. Ray kept saying, "The Shelley Russets are gonna clean right up." And Curtis loved being able to care about it all.

One afternoon late in the week Jay Stalworthy, Curtis' former boss, came huffing into the bedroom, hefting a T.V. set.

"What is that?" Curtis asked him. But he knew what it was.

"It's new," Jay said, as he set it so carefully down on the dresser. Then he plugged it in and adjusted it until the picture was perfect. "I knew you were going to be in trouble," he said as he turned around and grinned at Curtis, "not being smart enough to be able to work puzzles or read anything, so I brought you this."

They both laughed, and when Curtis held out his hand, Jay shook it slowly and with warmth. Curtis said, "Thanks," with love and appreciation in his eyes.

The next day, a week to the day since he had come home, Curtis was lying on his bed, watching his new T.V. and the L.A. Rams getting flattened by the Cowboys. Any other time, he would have loved it, but today, his right stump felt like a loaded pistol, about to go off. It was throbbing and hot, and the rest of his body felt as if he had the flush. Suddenly he felt something burst, and then there was a wetness down around the sore stump. He threw back the covers so he could take a look, and all at once, a horrible stench hit him.

He cried out, "Mom, Dad. . .I'm bursting open, I'm bursting open! You gotta help me!"

Later, the Brinkmans sat in the emergency waiting room of the Idaho Falls hospital. It was all too familiar a situation. When the doctor finally came in, they didn't rise, they didn't even look at him; they were too tired. They simply waited while he took a seat, not sure they wanted to hear what he would say.

"Well," he said finally, "I just don't know. There's a lot of infection there. I just don't know what's causing it. I'd like to keep Curtis here for a little while, a week or two. We'll use some antibiotics and heat, and I think things will clear up okay."

It wasn't bad news nor unexpected. They smiled and shook the doctor's hand and went home to gather their faith.

"Well, here I am, home again," Curtis mused, patting the little while metal table by his bed. He could have screamed out with anger and frustration, but by this time he knew that it would not help. At least he was closer to his family.

Two long weeks later, the infection was worse. The doctors were at a loss.

"This just shouldn't be, Curtis," Dr. Bjorenson said, gently probing the upper part of Curtis' right stump. "There's just got to be something up in there somewhere that's producing all of this infection. I think we really need to open it up and see what we can find. Can you handle that? We'd like to do that tomorrow morning."

"Fine, fine, anything to get this over with. Not that I don't like you guys or anything. I just hope I never see you again."

The next day started just the way every morning had for the last few months of Curtis' life. He was so familiar with pre-op procedures he could have instructed the nurses every step of the way. They put him out, and Dr. McCowen began his exploration. After a few minutes of deep probing, the doctor found something that was definitely out of place. He used the forceps, and he began to pull, gently. Finally, he drew it clear of Curtis' body. The staff all looked at each other in dismay, and the doctor whistled under his mask.

"Well, I'll be!" he said. "Will you look at that." Dangling from the forceps was a very soiled, very foul piece of limp gauze. It had evidently been left there after some previous operation and had kept things festering right along. They made a careful survey, determined that no such thing would happen again; then they cleaned and packed the wound and sent Curtis into the recovery room.

Shortly thereafter, Curtis was back in his room with his parents, and Dr. McCowen joined them, still in his green operating gown.

"Well, Curtis," he said, "there's good news, and there's bad news."

Curtis was still a little out of it. He said, "The bad first."

"Okay. The infection we couldn't get rid of was being caused by a gauze sponge somebody left inside you after an operation at the hospital in Salt Lake. It's really a shame that had to happen to you, but doctors are human like everybody else, and sometimes things go wrong. The good news is it's out, and you're on your way out of here."

Curtis was angry, even through the haze. The rest of the day he was angry. But by the time the afternoon was fading, he knew that he loved those people in Salt Lake for the work they'd done for him. It had been hard on everybody. Now, finally, that part of it was all over, and everything else was about to begin.

The infection cleared up. Curtis was in the hospital for some time after the operation, but he was healing, and that made things so much easier. One day he was taken into therapy where he was checked and weighed. "You're a big 73 pounds," the attendant told him, grinning in a friendly way.

"Not good," he mused, "but better. Better than in Salt Lake. At least I'm gaining." He got the nurse to leave him alone in there for awhile. He needed to do some checking of his own. Curtis waited until she was gone, then he took off his hospital gown and wheeled himself in front of the full-length mirror. His first thought when he finally saw himself was of those old paupers in India, the ones whose skin looks like ancient, wrinkled paper. He could see the bones where the skin was stretched tight over them. This is sickening, he thought. For the first time, he noticed how thin his cheeks were.

He put the gown back on. I never should have looked, he thought as he wheeled himself towards the door. Suddenly, it felt like there was a long, long way yet to go.

The next morning Dr. McCowen came in to pull the bandages packed on the open wounds of Curtis' leg. "It's looking good, Curtis," the doctor said, fiddling with some instruments.

By this time, Curtis knew more about pain than he had ever wanted to, and he kept an eye on the doctor as he was getting ready to do this last little operation, trying to figure out when the nurse was going to come give him a pain shot. Dr. McCowen was acting like he was pretty close to being ready to do it, and there was still nobody there to give Curtis anything for the pain.

"You're going to give me a shot, aren't you? A local or something?"

"Sure," the doctor said. "Oh, yeah." Then he started pulling. The pain was incredible. It felt like he was pulling forever, like there had to be three or four yards of packing up in there. Finally, it was over, and a nurse was giving him a shot. "Thanks, Doc," Curtis said. "I really appreciate it." He was thinking to himself, that after all I've been through, you'd think I could take a little horrible, excruciating pain for six seconds. I mean, what's six seconds of having your nerves shorted out?

Finally, there were only a few days left until Curtis could go home for good. He was sitting in his hospital room trying to think of ways to pass the time when he heard an outrageous bedlam in the hall. A circus maybe? he wondered. Then the door to his room gave way before a veritable panoply of people. They were all high school types, student body officers, cheerleaders — in uniform, no less — and a couple of standard, garden-variety kids, so he'd been at least partially right about the circus.

"Brinkman, Brinkman," they were saying all at once. "How ya doin'?" "You look awful." "You look great." "How can you stand it in here, it's so *clean!*"

It took Curtis a minute to get things in perspective.

"Since Mohammed would *not* come to the mountain. . . ," someone started. "Oh, Kent, you're so *educated*," someone remarked. "There was a pep assembly yesterday," one of the cheerleaders added, "and you were supposed to be like the guest of honor or something."

"And you didn't show. . . ," another student interjected.

"What a lousy way to get out of going back to school."

". . . so the pep assembly came to find you."

"And we brought the whole hot show for you, right here on this little old tape recorder."

". . . which doesn't work too good. . . ."

"And you are about to hear. . . ."

". . . maybe . . . ."

". . . the greatest . . . ."

"Would you guys just shut up and play the tape?"

"Play the tape!"

"We're now playing the tape." But nothing happened. Outside of the tape going around, there was nothing.

"Come *on!*" one of the cheerleaders said.

"I'm trying! I'm trying! Who recorded this?"

"You did, dork!"

"Well, ex-cuuuuse me!"

The up-shot of the whole thing was that no one got to hear the tape because there was evidently nothing on the tape. Curtis kept rolling his eyes and laughing, and everybody else was laughing, and the whole thing was really kind of stupid, which was just fine because that made it even better than it would have been.

When it was all over and the last cheerleader had exited out the door, Curtis shook his head, grinning. "That was so dumb," he thought. But it had made him feel pretty happy, even though he was so tired he could have died. Sleep came easily, especially because he wasn't really too worried about going back to school, now. It wasn't like his condition was going to be a shock to anybody at least. "All of a sudden I'm popular," he mused as he drifted off. "That's the way to do it; you wanna be popular, just go get your legs blown off. . .how stupid." But he went to sleep smiling.

Curtis' parents came to get him. This time he really was going home.

Actually, it was almost scary to leave the hospital this time.

He'd been psyched up for it last time, ready for all the hard things about adjusting to real life. Going back into the hospital had almost taken the spirit right out of him. He went home saying, "So what happens now?"

It was the middle of January. Curtis was sitting there by himself in front of good, old Shelley High School. It had been in May, the last day of school, since he'd gone through those doors. Who would ever have dreamed life could change so much so suddenly. "One summer. . . ," Curtis remembered, "one summer is all it took to make my life completely different. I used to run up and down those stairs without even thinking about it. Now, if I can get up over the curb, it'll be a miracle."

He wasn't actually alone. His dad was back in the car, making sure everything would be all right. But Curtis had wanted to accomplish this feat — going back — by himself, and his dad was more than content to let him try.

Somehow he did it. He got that wheelchair up to the door, and from there on it was only a matter of taking each task as it came to him. He had a lot of catching up to do. You don't miss the first three and a half months of school without feeling a thousand years behind.

But people helped. Teachers went easy, and he only had three or four classes, so it was okay.

He found that he was very concerned about what people would think when they saw him, so he had a wool blanket draped over the table to cover the place where his legs would have been, in hopes no one would notice that his legs were missing.

As time went by, the whole situation become a matter of fact. Everyone in school knew all about it, so he never had to face anyone's surprise. This all helped to make the transition from hospital to school very smooth.

One day Curtis' friends were taking him down the steps of the school on their way over to the seminary building. Also, there was a big assembly that was just starting in the auditorium behind them, and several grade school children were coming up the steps to attend it. Consequently, Curtis was in the middle of this huge mass of little children.

Kids are so frank. One of them took a good look at Curtis' chair, blanket and all, and said, "Hey, you don't have any legs down there." The rest of the children got interested, too, and were all asking, "What happened? How come you don't have any legs?"

Curtis was angry by the time he got down the stairs. Not at the kids — nor their questions — at himself. "This shouldn't get to me. Not by this time, it shouldn't." But it had gotten to him. When he'd left the hospital, he'd known about his legs. "How could you lose your legs and not *know* about it?" he fumed. But that's just how he felt when the kids had started noticing him, like he'd never really realized what had happened.

He thought about it. When Dr. Dean had come in to break it to him in the first place, Curtis had replied, "I understand, but I can't tell my folks. I just couldn't." So he'd asked the doctor to be the one to tell his folks, like they didn't already know. "The point is that I couldn't face that they'd taken off my legs. That's why I didn't want to tell my parents about it. If I had told them, I'd have had to believe it myself."

All the hours he'd spent "facing" it after that, all the resolution and the coming to grips with the future, the exercising of faith, even coming back to school — everyone had been so careful here not to look at him, not to say anything; everybody had treated him like nothing was different, like he'd simply been gone for awhile — nothing had prepared him for the fact that sooner or later a third grader would see him, notice (how could anyone ever really help but notice) and would say it out loud, "Hey, you don't have any legs."

So the blanket wasn't really hiding anything, and now it wasn't even hiding Curtis from himself. This emotional shock was a hard thing. But maybe it was the third grader that got him over the last big hurdle before he could really heal himself.

The rest of the year went mediocre. Curtis fought himself,

trying to forget what life used to be like, trying to feel normal. It wasn't easy. He had chucked the blanket, and that was a beginning. But now he had to take a completely different role in life, and that was hard. For one thing, he had loved basketball so much; sports like that can be the whole fabric of a kid's life. His friends included him. The coach had asked him to be the team manager, so he felt like he was doing something partly useful, but it was still very hard to sit there and watch everyone else play like he used to.

He went with them when they played games at other schools. The guys on the team helped transport him to games, to school, and to whatever else was happening. He warmed by degrees, reconciling himself to being a spectator, even though he hated it at first — so badly he could hardly take sitting there in that "stupid" chair.

His next hurdles were learning to drive with hand controls and how to use that *chair* that had to be his legs. All this, though, was teaching him to become more independent all the time. Nevertheless, Curtis had to fight his way through endless frustrations, and the only place he could vent his feelings was at home where they loved him no matter what. It ended up being his mother, the eternal scapegoat, who endured for the love of her boy.

Christmas came and went. For Curtis, it had always been a wonderful time, but this year it was more. He loved his family — even though there were days he didn't show it. After he'd been so close to death, when Christmas arrived, life and family took on a preciousness they'd never had before. It was a close time, a warm time.

After Christmas came the long stretch until the end of school. That was always a hard time anyway, with endless cold days and no holidays to speak of. He might have made things a little more interesting for himself by going out, but he just couldn't seem to find the courage to ask a girl. All the girls were friendly enough, but he couldn't help visualizing himself sitting through a whole dance watching everyone while the girl *pretended* to be having a nice time. Or what about that fact that she'd have to open doors for him? Even worse was imagining some girl's face when he asked her. She'd probably go just to be polite, but Curtis didn't want to take someone out just so she could feel sorry for him the whole time.

One day he was home watching the Houston Rockets play somebody, somewhere. The announcer was reeling off names, and they were flashing team pictures on the screen when suddenly Curtis yelled and pointed. Greg, his mouth full of toast, said, "What? What?" and all Curtis would say was, "I can't believe it! I can't believe it!" Finally, Greg got up and belted him one and said, "What?"

"I know that guy!" Curtis exclaimed.

"What guy?" Greg asked, understandably confused.

"That Mike Newlin guy they just showed. He was in the hospital with me. At the same time."

"Yeah?" Greg said.

"Yeah, he had an operation. . . ," Curtis said, and then sort of faded away, so Greg went back to his toast. Curtis was remembering how he thought that guy was so stupid, thinking he could ever play pro ball. But he did it. So things *did* happen like that. Things *could* happen.

Curtis started working a little harder at school. He was feeling guilty because he'd had it so easy for so long. In fact, he worked hard enough that he ended the year with a 4.0 GPA, and that really blew him away. The most amazing part of it was that he'd gotten an A in Algebra II. It wouldn't have been amazing for Smash Landon, but for Curtis it was like a major miracle.

As it got warmer outside and spring coming, driving everybody nuts the way it does, Curtis began to feel a little less awkward about being alive. His friends were just like they'd always been — Tony and Smash making a big contest about who could pop the longest wheelies in the wheelchair. That didn't go over very well with the teachers, since the boys were doing the wheelies down the main hall. Curtis started feeling a little more like he could be crazy, too. Things were getting more natural, not because everybody was trying to ignore Curtis' condition, just because they all, including Curtis, were beginning to accept it.

It got harder and harder for everybody to sit through class. The outside was too warm and too beautiful.

Curtis' little follow-up operations became less frequent, and there wasn't much pain left now. He was opening up with the rest of the world, emerging with the spring like a brand new creature, and he got stronger with every day that went by, his spirit stretching itself, remembering itself.

CHAPTER SIX
Acceptance

School was finally out. Two days later the Brinkmans all piled into the car and took Curtis away again, this time up to the Elks Rehabilitation Center in Boise. It was a five-hour trip, but since Curtis wasn't so sure he wanted to go, the hours went like lightning, so before actually realizing it, he was alone again, sitting at the front entrance waving goodbye from his wheelchair as the family car disappeared down the road.

"Come on, Curtis," he said, "everybody could use a little rehab." But it didn't make him feel any better, being in this strange place with people who were going to make him do hard things *for his own good*. "This isn't what I would have chosen to do with my summer," he chuckled. "I can just see it in English next fall, 'Write an essay of what you did last summer.' Oh, I spent it doing things *for my own good*."

Actually, Curtis didn't have a whole lot of time to feel sorry for himself. The staff just jumped right in on him, working away at whatever shell he had left, determined to make him blossom like the proverbial rose.

It was quite a place. There were nurses, occupational and physical therapists, technicians, and dozens of others, all well acquainted with people in Curtis' position, all skilled in dealing with those problems.

There was one cute little physical therapist that Curtis liked a lot. Her name was Arlee, and she was stronger than she looked. She demanded a lot from Curtis, but at the same time, she supported him and encouraged him. She called him Arms. "Hey, Arms," she would say, "over here." Later it was Tiger. That was the motivation Curtis needed — some cute little therapist calling him Tiger.

Motivation was the name of the game. The center and its programs were all aimed at pulling victims of tragic accidents out of their shock, confusion, and bitterness — at motivating them to approach life realistically and with confidence. These people usually found themselves without the ability to do the things that had been their whole lives before, leaving them feeling empty and useless. The center was there to show them what they *could* do.

Others were there, people like Curtis who had to find new lives and form new expectations for themselves. Bob was a twenty-nine year old logger when a tree had fallen on him, breaking his back and leaving him partially paralyzed. He had spirit and was determined to learn to use crutches. Another patient, Jim, who was only fourteen, had paralysis problems. The people who were there getting help were just like people everywhere, all different, all with needs, and the program was tailored to each one of them.

One of the activities Curtis began right away was basketball. He was put on a rickshaw affair, weighted in the back, then pushed out on the floor with a team. The game was played with a tiny ball. Curtis found that his hands still worked, that the skill that had always been in his hands was still there.

They played volleyball, too. This they played with a huge, featherweight ball. Curtis always chose to play on the team that had the least members so he could dominate the entire back line. The ball was slow enough that Curtis had time to maneuver his rickshaw around, feeling fast and rowdy as he came up under the ball, smacking it back over the net. He liked to set the ball up for the front zone so the people up there who had little arm control could hit it over, and every time he did, he learned that, even though he was partially disabled himself, there were people he could help, gaps he could fill.

It was like a balm to him, to be a part of the whole team situation, to function as a part of a unit, to belong and be useful.

There were others who could not play the games at all. One girl couldn't move anything but her head. She had learned to clench a stick between her teeth and type. The words she wrote were beautiful and artistic. She could hold a brush or a pencil in her teeth and draw, deftly putting forms on the paper or canvas, creating lovely pictures that overflowed with the life she could no longer express with her body.

Curtis watched her, and she amazed him. As he watched, he began to feel ashamed; she was so handicapped, but she could do so much. He had lost only his legs and could certainly do more. He began to explore new skills, such as putting charcoal to paper. Finding a talent that he'd never known was there was fulfilling and made him begin to grow.

The real education began when his new legs arrived. Curtis looked at them dubiously, then began handling them. He wasn't sure how they worked, and he was pretty sure he didn't want to find out. But the time came to try them on, so he didn't really have all that much to say about it.

First, he had to put an elastic "stumpsock" over each stump. Later, they'd teach him to use an ace wrap instead, but he had to begin with the basics. After he had the socks on, he had to fit his stump down into the hollow top of the leg; then there was a suction plug that had to be pushed into a hole at the knee. The pressure of the plug kept the stump down inside the leg.

"Now that I'm in, what do I do?" he asked. Arlee showed him. She indicated that he was to grab the rail next to him with one hand and take her hand with the other. Then they pulled. He pulled — she pulled. Gradually, he came upright. It was so weird being up there.

"This is like stilts or something. I feel like a heron," he said.

"Okay, Tiger," Arlee said, smiling at him. "You're up. Let's see you do some walking."

He rolled his eyes at her, but she only smiled as if to say, "I dare you." He grabbed the crutch she was holding out and kept a good grip on the rail; then he concentrated, flexing the muscles in his arms and shoulders in the strength of his effort. He swung one leg out. Then the other. He opened his eyes.

"Maybe they work," he said, like he was amazed.

"What do you mean, 'maybe'?" she said, cuffing his hair. "See? You've got legs again. Easy as that."

But it wasn't all that easy.

It took days before he really felt any confidence at all. The rehab patients worked in a room that had practice stairs and ramps in it, and no sooner had he learned to put one foot in front of the other, but there was Arlee, making him go up and down the stairs, up and down until he could get the hang of it, balancing out in the air on those legs. Then she put him on the ramp. Going up wasn't any problem at all. It was the coming down that got steep and scary. He concentrated so hard on keeping his balance that he almost forgot to make his legs take a step.

The legs had moveable feet, and the ankle joint was flexible. If he came down on the heel, the whole foot would make contact with the ground, then things would go along smoothly. If he came down wrong or if he lost balance — which at first was more the rule than the exception — he fell. By the end of those first few days he was a mass of bruises and sores.

The stumps hurt, too. Everytime he put the legs on he had to sit there for a minute, waiting out the pain, waiting until he could get used to the feeling. It took a lot of courage, getting up at the beginning of each session, but once he was there he worked hard, one step after another, trying to achieve some sort of natural motion.

Each session was two hours long, two hours of pain, frustration, failure, struggles, and success, which made it feel much longer. It was such a special relief to be able to pull the plug on those legs and head for occupational therapy or lunch.

As the days passed, Curtis made a lot of progress. One morning Arlee sat by him at breakfast.

"You're doing very well, Tiger," she said. "You know, I think that calls for a little celebration. So you know what we're going to do?" She smiled at him innocently enough, but Curtis knew by now how to tell when something rotten was going to happen. "We're going to take you out into the real world and give Tiger Brinkman a chance to see what it's like to be just as tall as everybody else."

All he could do was shake his head in dread of whatever it was she had planned.

After breakfast, Arlee helped him into the rehab van.

"You want to at least tell me where it is you're taking me?" he asked, alarmed to see they were heading right out of Boise.

She looked over at him, then back at the road, and she smiled again, arching her eyebrows. She answered, "You see those planes landing over there? That, my friend, is where we're going. Sound like fun?"

It took some comprehension. He looked at her like he couldn't believe what he was seeing.

"And I thought you were human," he said. "Under that cute little exterior there's some kind of fiend. You've got to be kidding. Do you really expect me to go into the airport and get mashed in there with all those people who are all in a hurry, where you could get knocked over and trampled even if you had your normal legs, only I'll be on those stilts of mine? Come on, Arlee — you know we don't even practice outside because if the wind came up, I'd be a goner. You know I'll fall — in front of all those people."

"So, who will know you? What do you care?"

He shook his head; he was through trying to kid her out of it. "I really don't think I'm ready for this," he said, and he was pleading because you just can't tell a therapist what you'll do and what you won't; they're too noble for that. "Let's wait a week, okay, Arlee? A week?"

She looked at him again. There was something awfully final in the way she was smiling. "I'll be with you the whole time," she said. And that was that.

The doors into the terminal swung open all by themselves, and there was Curtis Brinkman, standing there, looking at the incredible crowd of people inside, all in a hurry to get somewhere, just like he said they'd be. "Go on," Arlee said from behind him, so he did. But he was using crutches and had fake legs, which made everybody stare at him. Suddenly he felt like he had no clothes on and just wanted to go away.

Arlee gave him a gentle push. "Over there," she said, pointing at the escalator.

"Come *on!*" he said to her, but she just kept pushing. So he moved. He watched those little steps flipping up from under the floor, one after another, so quick, so rapid, and he kept inching closer to them. Finally, he was standing right smack in front of the stairs and watching them was making him dizzy.

"Up," she said. He tried to look at her over his shoulder, but all he saw was that people were starting to line up behind him. The stairs never stopped moving, and the people just kept lining up — the pressure was unreal.

"I'm with you," she said. "Terrific," he retorted. He put his weight on the crutches and moved one foot out, trying to time the stairs right. That foot made it and started up, leaving the rest of his body right where it was. He said, "Wait," and he pulled the foot back in before it could get too far away from him.

"I have two feet down there," he said, "both of which are slower than these stairs." He was burning with embarrassment. "Just hold it a minute," he hissed at the stairs.

"Curtis," she said from behind him, "the world can't always tailor itself to what you think you need."

Curtis' jaw tightened. He gripped the crutches, pushed off, and swung his legs forward, more or less vaulting onto the escalator. He made it! Then, he had to get off, but that was like a picnic compared to what he'd just been through.

Arlee caught his arm before he could get away from her. and she turned him around. "Down," she said. He looked down from where he was standing, and even being four feet away from being able to look straight down the stairs made his stomach turn. "Forget it," he said. "We'll take the elevator."

She had that mule look, and he knew he was doomed. "Really, Arlee," he said, pleading again, "I don't even do well on the ramp in therapy, and it doesn't move." But it was no good. He could have kicked her. "All right, all right," he said, "if it makes you happy, I'll go kill myself for you."

He moved himself over to the head of the escalator, and this time he didn't look at it long enough to psyche himself out before he jumped on. He made it again. But going down still wasn't as secure as going up had been. The whole way down he felt like he was leaning too far forward, like he was going to end up on his face any minute, even with his crutches.

It scared him so bad, feeling so off balance, a fall really was inevitable. It happened right down near the bottom. He panicked and lost control. Down he went, grabbing, scrambling, and taking the guy in front of him down with him. The people behind him turned around and kept trying to climb back up the escalator to avoid the mess on the floor, but there were people behind them, and pretty soon the entire situation looked like a scene from the "Keystone Kops"!

Finally, someone moved Curtis out of the way but not far enough that he couldn't catch all the comments as people went by. Some of them were pretty humorless.

"Sir," someone said. Curtis looked up, and there was a ground steward leaning over him. "There *is* an elevator over there." Curtis just looked up at him from the floor. Then he looked around for Arlee, who, of course, was nowhere to be seen.

"Yes, I know," Curtis said to the man. "I am learning to use these," he indicated the legs and the crutches with a sweep of his hand, "and I have to do things like this *for my own good*." He was speaking very politely. If Arlee were close enough to hear, she'd know how mad he was.

"Well, we still would invite you to use the elevator."

"Thank you," Curtis said, a mite dryly.

"I'll be right with you the whole time," Curtis said to Arlee as she helped him up, having reappeared somewhat conveniently, he thought, after all the people had gone away.

"You did great," she said. He just smiled at her like he'd much rather belt her one and headed out to the van.

She told the whole story at dinner. Curtis was sure he'd be utterly mortified if anyone he knew ever heard about the whole thing, but by the time she got to the end of the story, he was laughing his head off just like everybody else.

After that, he felt relieved, as though a big weight had been lifted from him. "See, no one spits at cripples anymore," Arlee had said. And in more than one way, she was right.

He kept practicing. He had a problem with arching his back too much, overcompensating while he was searching for balance. But eventually, the arch began to go away, because he was gaining control. Once, when he was frustrated to death, he said, "Why me? Why did this whole rotten thing happen to *me*?" Arlee had looked at him coolly and said, "Because you were the one stupid enough to climb the power pole." She was right. He had no excuses for his anger; there was no one to blame but himself, no one he could use to justify his failure. This thought kept him working.

In occupational therapy he made a wooden case for his legs. He sanded it, varnished it, and when it was finished, he liked it. It was nice to accomplish something tangible. It gave him a little more confidence.

He continued learning to drive with the hand controls. At first, he'd had a hard time believing they could really work very well, but after he had almost thrown his instructor through the windshield by squeezing a little too hard on the power brake control, Curtis figured he could be just as safe a driver with his hands as most people were with their feet. The instructor might have had some thoughts of his own about that, but Curtis did finally get his driver's license, and that went a long way towards making him feel like a man.

He stayed at the center for only a month, a short time really. The amount of learning he had experienced there made him feel very attached to the place. It was almost like a home to him because he loved so many people there. It was hard for him to leave, but not because he felt unready to re-enter the world. The people at the center had given him his parting gift: confidence, courage, and imagination.

One of the first things Curtis wanted to do when he got home was walk from his house right down into town; it had been many months since he'd been able to do that on his own two legs. So his first day home he left the house and swung himself across the yard. Curtis ducked as he went under the rose-covered arch over the gate, not because he needed to, but because he *wanted* to need to.

He traveled east to the highway, where he stopped to catch his breath and adjust things, then headed north towards the center of town. By the time he made Huntsman's Food Town, Curtis was about exhausted. He leaned against the wall a minute. Two of his school friends came out of the store just then, eating donuts and laughing at something that must have been very funny. Then they saw Curtis.

"Curtis, you've got legs!" one of them said. "Where'd you get legs?"

"Yeah, you look like yourself again, almost. How does it feel?"

Curtis smiled at them, forgetting how tired and sore he was. "They take some getting used to. But it sure beats sitting around on my duff all the time." He noticed that they had to look up at him. That was nice. He'd lost a few inches — he was only 6'2" with these legs — but he was still taller than most, and he liked that feeling, even if his arms did look a little longer than they did before.

He started moving again, and this time he made it all the way to the Shelley library. But that was it. His stumps were killing him, and he was exhausted, so somebody called Curtis' mom, who drove right out and picked him up. She had a hard time not making too big a deal out of how wonderful she felt, how proud she was of him.

That's much the way the rest of the summer passed; Curtis doing new things, learning, using his legs, trying to overcome the pain that sometimes bothered him. He developed sores on his stumps from using the legs so much, and the legs were hard on his other skin grafts, too, but he just kept working at it. He still worried about the future but less than before. There was more to do now; less time for worry.

School started again, and Curtis was a senior. The year passed fairly quickly, as senior years do. Curtis was still managing the team, so he got to travel a lot. He was also an active Priest in the LDS Church. All in all, his social confidence was slowly growing.

More operations were performed on his stumps, making the legs easier to use, even though they were still painful, and he occasionally went through bouts with depression and frustration. Curtis worked out a lot and put on weight, but he still didn't feel genuinely strong or productive. His life made him almost seasick he'd been up and down so much; one minute he was totally ready for life, the next he just wanted to go to bed and forget the whole thing.

Graduation came. It was probably no more frightening for Curtis to graduate than for any other high school senior, waking up the next morning and realizing that now he had to *do* something with himself. Those summer days went so fast. And late at night, out in the backyard under the stars, the class of '72 got together to plan each other's lives, talking out the possibilities, throwing out ideas, dreaming in the cool summer grass.

Some of Curtis' friends who were working at the French's potato processing plant that summer planned to keep their jobs until they got old enough to leave on missions. Some of the guys were going to go to college — Ricks or B.Y.U. There were others who were either going to stay and take over the family farms someday or who were going to work, get married, and have kids — but what was Curtis going to do? He really didn't know, and it began to get him down.

He had thought about careers. One of his friends was going into accounting, which could be done with no legs, he thought, but only if you *had* to. He couldn't even feel good about leaving home in general, much less having to be on his own, making a living. This having to decide was making him nervous.

Altogether, Curtis had worked himself into a sort of mental limbo; he couldn't decide on anything. What he seemed to do best was get discouraged.

One day his folks announced that the old black willow in the backyard had to go. It was just like saying, "Well, let's go out and shoot Rover." That tree had been everything to everybody; jungle, airplane, tent, you name it. It was older than anyone could guess, but the bugs had finally gotten it.

When it had been felled and the gigantic trunk had been made into a years' supply of firewood, there was nothing left but the mammoth stump and the incredible root system. "Poor old tree," Curtis mused, looking at it one day. "Both of us, just stumps." There had been a lot of talk about how to get the stump out of the yard. The folks were thinking that maybe they would hire somebody with a tractor or grader or something to come pull the thing out. But it came to Curtis as he was standing there, feeling sorry for both the tree and himself, that *he'd* like to dig it all up. It was like he owed the tree that much. He talked it over with Greg, and they presented the idea to their dad who was more than a little dubious at first.

"We can do it, Dad. We really can."

"Well, you know, you two. . .just like anything else I've ever had you do, if you start this project, you'll have to finish it. You honestly want to take it on?"

They did. So he let them. And it turned out to be a lot harder than they'd counted on. They worked for three weeks, digging until their blisters turned into callouses, before they finally unearthed the base of the trunk. The roots that came off were more like branches they were so thick, and the boys spent two more weeks chopping and digging, chopping off the roots with hatchets and digging to expose more of the root system.

What they ended up with after five weeks was a hole about fifteen feet wide and five feet deep with the stump squatting right down in the middle of things. Curtis felt like he was in an underground cavern when he went down in the hole. He'd hold up his stumps and walk around on his hands. By doing this it made him small enought to fit in the holes under the roots, and even down under the stump itself. He felt like some kind of hobbit, being so small in those damp holes that smelled richly of dirt.

The best part was that he was working his head off, getting totally dirty, getting really tired from doing real work. Chopping and digging away at his own life had been hard because he could never see what progress he had made, but this was different. He could see every inch of his work, every minute of it, and it was so good to know this was a problem that could be solved.

The day they finally pulled that stump free from the ground was Curtis' day. It was the same feeling he'd experienced when he left the rehab center; he knew he could do things, and he was in the mood to try.

In that spirit Curtis decided he would study business at Boise State. He chose Boise specifically because the land was flat, the weather was good, and the campus was beautiful. He was ready to get on with his life, to start a career, to make something happen. He was on his way.

CHAPTER SEVEN
Greg

Curtis sat at his tiny desk, chin in hand, gazing out the dorm window, out over the campus, out over the edge of the world. He was in a gazing mood. He'd been studying hard, and his mind needed a stretch, so he just put his eyes on auto pilot and let his thoughts wander. After awhile, he started to whistle a little. The whistle made him smile, it was such a pleasant thing. Eighteen years of his life he'd spent not being able to whistle, then he'd gone to college and finally learned how. That's why I was meant to come here, he thought. I needed to learn to whistle. . . .

He'd been at school now a couple of weeks or more. It seemed like a short time and like forever, all at once. He thought about his schedule; English was required, but that wasn't too bad. Accounting was okay, and psychology was actually interesting. He was doing all right so far with keeping up. The only really tough class he had was algebra, but that didn't surprise him.

It was a nice campus. It had ramps almost every place, so he could get around easily enough. He had an electric cart he rode around that enabled him to get right up next to a building, then put his legs on to walk inside, so life was reasonably comfortable for Curtis. There had been some hairy moments at first, before he grew used to everything. One time he'd misjudged his speed and sent his power buggy right through a glass door. That was a mess, and he'd been worried about the school's reaction, but everything worked out fine. The administrator he'd talked to had been very good to him.

Actually, just about everybody he met had been kind to

him. He thought about the people who had become his friends. They weren't what he'd expected to find. He'd expected to find the Mormon kids right away; he was used to them — he'd grown up with them. But the only Mormon he could find was a long-hair who smoked and who didn't give one hoot about either Curtis or the Church. That didn't hurt Curtis' feelings though. The guy wasn't exactly his type.

He found that time and circumstance crystalized friendships quite naturally, and soon he knew a whole group of people who were a lot like him: fun, moderate, nice, even though they weren't Mormon. He'd been afraid that non-Mormon people would pressure him into all kinds of things he didn't want to do, but that just didn't happen. His friends respected the way he felt about things, always tolerant of him, and he found that he respected them, too.

It was there at Boise State that he met his first black friend. At first, Curtis was a little afraid of him, not knowing how to talk to someone who seemed so different. But he began to see that this person was only a lonely human being who was just as homesick and just as worried about being different as Curtis was himself. They became good friends, spending a lot of time facing one another across a chess board.

There was a Hawaiian that Curtis liked a lot. The fellow was one of those health-minded people who ate only the right things, so he didn't have one bit of trouble with the fact that Curtis did not drink or smoke. He had fuzzy red hair, and Curtis thought he had a great personality.

There were others, and it was nice to be involved with them, nice to have somebody to care about. Life was comfortable at Boise State, and that made the future look very accessible.

He had thought a lot about home. I was so scared to leave there, he thought. But now he felt independent; he didn't need to be home anymore. In fact, one weekend when he could have gone home, he didn't. Some of his friends from Blackfoot had offered him a ride. He thought maybe he'd go, and he'd written his parents, telling them to expect him, but the day before they were going to leave he felt like he just had too much studying to do. The fact was that he was having too much fun being where he was, and he felt that the trip was too long and the stay too short for him to justify going.

He was thinking that Thanksgiving would arrive before he knew it, and there would be plenty of time for going home. He hoped his folks would understand. Anyway, he was still mad at Greg. They had a big knock-down-drag-out fight the day before he left, and Greg hadn't really apologized yet for being such a horse's tail. He will, Curtis thought. I may not be as big as I was, but I'm still older than he is.

Somebody knocked at the door. It startled Curtis, and he knocked a book off the desk with his elbow. "What?" he yelled, picking the book up.

"Come on, Brinkman," somebody yelled. "We're going over to check out the chicks at the T.V. room. You comin'?"

"I'm comin'," he said, swinging himself off the chair, dropping easily into his wheelchair. His arms were getting strong. "I've got to get my jacket," he yelled. "I'm not as hot blooded as some people." They laughed as he opened the door; then they all headed off to the Student Union building.

Richard Clark stood in the entryway of the Student Union. He was an impressive man, with a solemn face, dressed in a dark business suit. He had spent considerable time tracking Curtis down, but now that he had found him he was somewhat reluctant to do what he must.

He was Curtis' mother's cousin and lived in Boise. That's why he had to be the one to find Curtis. There was a message he had to deliver.

Richard moved down the hallway to the T.V. room. He stopped in the doorway and glanced around the room, searching for Curtis. Moving across the room, around chairs, excusing himself as he passed in front of small groups of students, they all turned to look at him, not only because his appearance was so unusual for the time and place but also because there was something in his face that seemed to trouble him.

"Curtis," he said as he put his hand on Curtis' shoulder. "I am your mother's cousin, Richard Clark."

Curtis turned and looked at him, surprised. He held out his hand and began to smile, but something in the man's eyes kept him from it.

"I need to speak with you privately, if I may, Curtis," he said.

They left the room. There was a lounge just down the hall, and it was empty. That's where they went. "Please, sit down," Curtis said, but the man only smiled a tight little smile and remained where he was.

"I have to tell you, Curtis. . .your mother phoned me an hour or so ago. She wanted me to find you and let you know that your brother has been in an accident. It was with a spud combine."

Curtis looked at the man's face and suddenly chilled. "It'll be all right. Greg's very tough," he said.

"He wasn't hurt too badly, was he?" Even then Curtis knew.

The man looked so sad. "Curtis, I hate to be the one who has to tell you this. It was very bad. He was killed, Curtis."

"Greg?" Curtis said, like there was some other brother, like the whole thing could be — must be — a mistake. He searched the man's face, he didn't even know what for. The man wanted to touch him or say the right thing, but there was no right thing to say. Curtis already knew what death meant; he had been prepared by his church with knowledge and hope, but then, always in the abstract, never because someone had died. "No," Curtis said, tears swelling up in his eyes.

"You are booked onto a flight that will leave in half an hour, Curtis. I will take you to the airport, if you like." But Curtis wasn't hearing. He was on his way back to his room to pack, and all the man could do was follow and hope he could help.

Curtis put his legs on. He was trying to understand that the situation was real, but he just couldn't come to terms with it — it was too unbelievable. He thought he should be crying, but he wasn't. He didn't even feel sorrow yet. It had been too much of a shock. "This is stupid," he said. "If anyone was going to die, it should have been me. Why wasn't it me?" His hands were shaking.

It was a hard flight home.

His parents were there to meet him. His father's face was full of grief, and his mother was crying, but he couldn't show any emotion. Tony had come with them. It seemed that whenever there was trouble, Tony was there, helping.

Curtis embraced his parents, consoling them, commiserating. But to Tony he asked, "Is it true?" And it was only then that the awful reality of Greg's death hit him full in the face. "Oh, Greg," he cried. "Oh, dear Lord, please no."

Tony stayed late that night, talking to Curtis. Tony told him how it happened. Greg had been behind the combine, pulling at something that was stuck. The combine driver hadn't known he was there, and when he started the machine up, it had pulled Greg right in. That was it.

Curtis didn't ask who the driver had been. He never wanted to know. It was okay to hate somebody as long as you didn't know who it was.

The whole thing had happened only a few hundred yards from where Curtis' accident took place. It was strange, almost spooky. Tony finally went home, and Curtis went to bed. He left a light on just for comfort.

It was a bad night. He tossed and turned and couldn't stop his mind; it just kept going over the same ground again and again. About halfway through the night, he was horrified to remember the fight they'd had before he left for college. They *had* made up, a little. But wasn't it this afternoon that Curtis had still been mad? It seemed like a million afternoons ago, now. So what if Greg had been hard to get along with sometimes? It was only because he was growing up. Curtis should have been kinder. He should have loved Greg more, should have said it more.

What if he'd come home for the weekend like he was going to? Maybe Greg wouldn't have gone to work that day. Then they would have been together, and he wouldn't have been killed. If he'd just not been so self-centered about staying in school. . . .

Yes, it was a bad night.

Curtis stood in the line, shaking endless hands of friends and relatives until he could have screamed. All of the people were kind, sorry, and consoling, but he didn't want to see them, didn't want to keep having to talk about the tragedy. The people were here to share his grief, but grief is a very private thing, and Curtis didn't want to have to share it with anybody but his family.

He looked over at his mother. She was holding up, but it wasn't easy for her either. She was one person he very much wanted to share his emotion with, but there was still no outward show in Curtis, just this aching, horrible confusion and loss, all dammed up somewhere in his chest.

The last person went through the line and left. They closed the door, and the family was alone. Curtis' father closed the viewing with a family prayer, which Curtis could only barely hear through his anguish. After the "amen," the family members began to slowly move, getting themselves ready to go to the chapel for the funeral. But Curtis couldn't move. "This isn't the time," he wrestled with his emotions. "First, I can't even cry, and now when I need to be strong for everybody else, I'm losing it. I can't lose it. . . ." By that time he was already crying. He couldn't stop; it was like he was drowning in his grief and couldn't control it.

They all took care of him. He cried until his nose bled. Then it was time to go, so he cleaned himself up and followed everyone in.

It was a beautiful funeral. It was hard for the family, but Curtis knew that Greg was all right. He knew there was an afterlife. But then he'd remember the unrelenting fact that Greg wouldn't be there to talk to, laugh with, or beat on, and it was nearly too hard.

A few days later Curtis went back to Boise. He didn't feel much like going. He didn't feel much like talking to anyone, having to care about anybody, and he didn't want to explain what had happened. He isolated himself so effectively that some of his friends didn't even know he was back. He stayed in his room, didn't eat, didn't do anything, but work up a deep depression.

"What's the use," he kept saying to himself. And then he finally decided to go home. He knew his parents wouldn't like it, but he couldn't accomplish anything at Boise in his state of mind, and he didn't foresee a change in that. Anyway, he needed his family. He needed them to be close. So he went home after a week of nothing.

But there was nothing at home either. All he did was hang around until he'd driven everyone in the house—including himself—berserk. His parents had done everything in the world they could think of to bring him out of it. His two little sisters, Katherine and Ellen, tried until they were almost as depressed as he was.

The Brinkmans were at their wits' end. They had lost one son, almost lost the other. Now the one who had made it was fading on them again. It just couldn't go on this way. They prayed their hearts out. They talked about it and talked about it, trying to find a way to help him.

It was still fall, and the spud harvest was going strong. Curtis couldn't stand the four walls anymore; he was too used to being out, working the season through. His body was one big, immobile cramp, and he couldn't stand it. He put himself into his wheelchair and got out of the house.

Curtis went out on the road. He was taking himself somewhere, anywhere, the energy of his frustration pushing him, pushing him further and faster. He wheeled down Shelley's Main Street, past King Drug, past the library, past everything and then out into the country. He gripped the wheels, pushing them down hard, like he was trying to push them away, and climbed a little hill.

Sweat was dripping into his eyes, reminding him of the day he and Greg worked with the old willow tree. He then pushed himself out to the familiar farm area. By the time he reached

Searle's his body was exhausted, soaked with sweat, and the blisters worn on his hands were open and stinging. But the unused anger was still there.

He topped a rise and sat there, watching the work as it went on in the fields. The boys who were following the combines and working the cellars could have been any of a hundred he had known; it could have been himself out there, or Greg, before things had changed. He thought about those old days, about working on a team, about the crazy things they had done and the big machines they had run, and it only made him angrier.

He turned the chair around to begin going home. Where else would he go? He was going a lot slower now and breathing harder. He left the road at the gravel pits, wrenching the chair over the rocks until he found himself in a little private place between the mounds of gravel and the river.

He thought about Greg. And his anger surged. It was God he was mad at he decided. "Why didn't you warn me?" he shouted, crying. "You're supposed to be such a God of love and miracles. I could have saved him if you'd have warned me." He shouted like he was trying to make sure God could hear, telling God the whole thing didn't make any sense. He shouted, cried, and shook his fists at the heavens until he couldn't do any more, and then he cried even more. Later, he took himself out of the pits, back up onto the road, and went home.

His parents had come to a decision. They *were* his parents, after all, and if he was going to play the helpless little child, they were going to act accordingly. They knew that this inactivity was killing his mind, and they determined that he no longer would be inactive.

"Curtis," his father said. "There will be an end to this. You have to shake this thing off and get your life moving again. We have talked to some people at Ricks College, and we can get you in on their block plan. It's what we want you to do. It's what you need. We are asking you to go."

Curtis thought about it. Ricks was at Rexburg, not too far from home. If he didn't like it, it would be easy enough for him to retreat. He couldn't really decline on the basis that he had anything more important to do. So, in the end, he went.

CHAPTER EIGHT
A New Life

Mark Etherington would have been a calming influence on anybody. He had an air of quiet maturity, due, perhaps in part, to the fact that he was already slightly balding. He had just returned from an LDS mission, was about twenty-two, and was Curtis' roommate at Ricks College.

Mark was the elder's quorum president in the student ward, and that meant he had the responsibility of keeping his eye on the welfare of all the young men in the congregation. Because he was essentially calm and serious and because of his sensitive nature, he did the job very well.

One responsibility he took very seriously was his roommate, Curtis. He could sense the wound that was there, and he quietly went about treating it. It wasn't in him to preach or to push; he had too much genuine compassion for that. So he simply loved Curtis right back into the old, comfortable relationship Curtis had enjoyed with the Lord. Mark taught him to understand, to pray, and to be part of the Church, but never asked him to disregard his anger — he just taught him how to deal with it.

The ward was divided into smaller units of about twenty people called "family home evening" groups, the purpose of which was to provide some substitute for the family involvement the students were missing at college. The groups encouraged friendships and personal involvement and allowed a bit of an escape from the more serious aspects of school in a relaxed social situation. In other words, Curtis and his roommates and some friends got together with a group of girls on a regular weekly basis, and the whole bunch of them had some good, clean fun.

Mark was the leader of their particular group, and he made sure that every activity they planned was geared to Curtis. Once they considered roller skating, and since the problem with that, as far as Curtis was concerned, was obvious, they went bowling instead. Occasionally, Curtis chafed under that kind of attention, but he was wise enough to understand that love and not pity was behind it, so he endured.

Curtis began to grow again. He had done some regressing as far as his attitudes towards himself and his life went, so his first period of growth was more like regrowth. He had to accept himself again, rebuild his confidence.

The relationships he formed with the others on his dorm floor were most therapeutic. It was like living with forty brothers around, and that in itself was soothing. The boys did a lot of talking and praying together, reinforcing one another spiritually. But they were boys, and most of the time they kept themselves busy with crazy things, gleefully torturing each other, and generally keeping life in the dorm on a very colorful level.

One of the pastimes in which they took great delight was "tubbing." Tubbing was a matter of dumping someone, anyone, into a tub full of very cold water or snow when they could get it. They took a kind of Roman pleasure in the thing, and they did it whenever they had the slightest justification.

Once they grabbed one of Curtis' favorite friends, Russ, and were in the act of hauling him down to the tub when his supplications reached Curtis who was studying in his room. Curtis had a tender heart. In a matter of moments he had swung himself off the chair, across the floor, and out into the hallway on his hands. Nobody was expecting an attack from below, so Curtis caught them all off guard, by the ankles. Pretty soon the hall was a mass of struggling, punching, yelling college men, Curtis Brinkman right on the top of the pile, riding it like a wave. Russ was spared.

The year went along, and Curtis did well in his classes. His shyness began to wear off, and he even became brave enough to go out a few times — with girls! He could get around just fine, being strong as a horse, and there were a lot of people he loved.

At the end of the year, when it came time for the boys to say goodbye, they cried. Curtis' parents had done the right thing, sending him away to Ricks. Their decision had been a lot like the one Dr. Allen had made at LDS hospital in Salt Lake City. They had all known instinctively that the only way to heal a human being is to find a way to get him involved with someone else; man was never built to survive with only himself for companionship.

The summer passed rapidly, and when the fall rolled around again, Curtis was ready and willing to head right back to school.

Before he'd left school in the spring, he had applied to be a resident assistant for men's housing. At that time, Mr. Miller, the housing coordinator, had told him not to count on the position, and Curtis wondered if it was because of his youth, or his handicap. But in late August, they contacted him, letting him know that the position was his — it was like an omen.

So he began the year herding his rowdy little flock along, making sure they changed their sheets once a week and listening to their sorrows. It was very good for him to take care of someone else; it made him grow up a little more.

Before too long Curtis found himself involved in student government. He was the assistant to the Ombudsman; he sat on two student government committees and co-chaired another. He was on the standards committee and took a very active part in his ward. He was a very busy young man.

One weekend early in the year Curtis went to one of the first dances in the Manwaring Center ballroom. He didn't really mind not being able to dance; it was good to sit in the balcony talking to people and watching everyone else on the floor. He had parked his wheelchair and was sitting on the couch with some friends of his. It was like a big reunion, seeing all of these people from last year, and there were familiar faces all over the place.

Some girls were coming up the stairs just as Curtis was

turning that way to say "Hi" to someone. He recognized the girls, or at least most of them, from the year before. They came up to talk, and he greeted them all by name, asking how they'd been doing — how they'd spent the summer. He was very comfortable now with folks he knew, but he was still shy of new people, so he just pretended that the one girl he didn't know wasn't really there.

Oh, he noticed her all right. It was hard not to, with her beautiful eyes and infectious smile. But he didn't say a word to her, and she very understandably wrote him off as being rather stuck on himself; she did concede to herself, however, that he was very handsome, and she had a hard time erasing him from her mind.

The following Sunday Curtis discovered the "new girl" was in his ward, and she had at this point decided she could give him a second chance; after all, he *was* a friend of her sister's, and it *was* her duty to be nice.

Then came Monday night, and they also discovered they were in the same family home evening group. Curtis was the group leader, and DeAnne, her sister, was the hostess. That's where Curtis casually found out that her name was Bonnie — Bonnie Hymas, and that she was a P.E. major, although she didn't look like what he expected a P.E. major to look like.

It was an informal meeting that night, everybody introducing themselves, telling a little about themselves. Curtis had worn his legs that night, but Bonnie wasn't really noticing that kind of detail. When it came time for closing prayer and everyone else had knelt down easily, Curtis struggled down to his knees, and Bonnie watched him. She was feeling a very powerful spirit there, and she wondered what kind of a man he really was.

Curtis was so busy he could hardly keep track of the days; consequently, he didn't have a lot of time for socializing, and that fact, coupled with his bashfulness, made him almost a monk those first few weeks. So Bonnie ended up going out with Curtis' good friend and roommate, Alan Reddekopp. Alan was very nice, but he wasn't quite what she had in mind.

What she had in mind was Curtis, so when he spoke in Sunday School one Sunday, and she had an excuse, she asked Alan to formally introduce her. She told Curtis that she liked his talk, but she was feeling like an idiot while she said it because she was really meaning something else. And she knew Alan was standing there trying to figure out why she wanted to meet Curtis at all.

It wasn't much, but it was enough of a meeting that Curtis felt brave enough to say "Hi" when he'd run into her on campus or at church. A few weeks after that, he stopped her on campus and asked her if she minded blind dates. She was hoping maybe this was one of those creative approaches, but it turned out he really did have a friend coming in from Shelley. She told him she'd have to meet the date first, and as Curtis began to wheel away, he said that was just fine.

"At least now I know he knows I'm female," she sighed. "I wonder if I should feel encouraged?"

Curtis still had to have special check-ups and adjustments from time to time. In October he needed to have his legs worked on, and he had to go to Boise to have the work done. It was a six-hour drive, and when he told his folks about it on the phone, they said no way was he going that far without taking somebody with him.

"That's a long drive, Curtis," his father said. "What if you should have car trouble or something? You'd be out there in the middle of nowhere in your wheelchair. That's not a good idea."

Well, his father was usually right, so Curtis promised he'd find somebody. He asked Alan, but he couldn't go because he had a big exam. He asked everybody he knew, and nobody could go. He was about to give up when Alan said, "Hey, call DeAnne and those guys. They'd probably love to go with you. You could probably get the whole apartment to go."

It took a great deal of persuasion to get Curtis to call the girls. In fact, Alan had to dial the phone for him. When someone finally answered the phone and he had explained the situation, there was only one girl who could really spare the time. It was Bonnie. Even after he told her they had to leave at four in the morning, she said she'd go. He thought she was nuts but was grateful.

Actually, Bonnie didn't really know anything about Idaho, being from Denver. She was assuming that Boise was maybe an hour from Rexburg, and she couldn't figure out why they had to leave so early. She shrugged philosophically, set her alarm, and got her clothes out before she went to bed so she could be sure she wouldn't end up wearing something weird.

Of course, she slept right through the alarm. It was the phone that awakened her.

She was standing there in her bathrobe, sleepy-eyed and tousled, holding the phone and listening to Curtis say, "I'll be there in two minutes. You ready?" She turned around, making a face at herself in the mirror; then she replied, "Yes, I'm ready."

When he pulled up in her parking lot, there she was, looking like an advertiser's dream. Curtis thought early mornings looked very good on her but only said, "Hi. How are you? Here we go," feeling very stupid.

They got up on the highway and were travelling along pretty fast. There was no traffic to speak of due mostly to the early darkness. There was nothing to see out the windows and weren't even any headlights coming their way. All they had was each other. And neither of them knew what to talk about.

"Bonnie," Curtis said finally, because somebody had to say something. He wondered what he was going to ask her. She was looking at him, her eyebrows raised, waiting. "Bonnie," he said, speaking in scholarly tones, "tell me, what is your philosophy of life?"

She laughed, and she thought what a corny question. Then she said, "You really want to know?"

He looked at her a minute through the dark; then he realized he did want to know. "Yes," he said, and he was serious. "Tell me."

It was miles later before they were aware of the passing time.

Bonnie looked at her watch and exclaimed, "My word, where *is* Boise?"

"You really don't know?" he said. Then he laughed. "You'd better relax. You've got another five hours ahead of you before we even see it."

The sun finally rose and rolled out over the wide Idaho plain. Curtis pointed out the sites as they passed them, the Craters of the Moon National Park, cities like Burley, and Twin Falls with its remarkable gorge.

Finally Bonnie pointed at the city they were approaching. "Boise?" she asked.

Curtis smiled. "Mountain Home. Boise is bigger. It's just on the other side of this one, so we're almost there, honest."

They did get to Boise and made his appointment right on time. Then Curtis showed Bonnie the town and the university. As he pointed out his old dorm, he thought about all the things that had happened since he'd lived there, and he was glad to be where he was now.

They went to lunch in a small, out of the way restaurant, and in the course of their conversation, Curtis looked at Bonnie seriously. There was something he found that he needed to know.

"Bonnie," he said, and his tone made her look up. "Are you — I just want to know, so tell me the truth — are you uncomfortable being with me, the way I am? I mean, does it make you feel uncomfortable being seen with me?"

She just looked at him, and he was suddenly afraid.

"Don't be stupid," she said. "Do you think I would have come if I felt like that?"

Curtis smiled. As he ordered some dessert, she studied his face. So he was self-conscious about his legs. She narrowed her eyes, examining her own feelings. She really hadn't thought much about that part of him, and now that surprised her. It probably should make a difference to me she thought, but she just couldn't seem to let it worry her. She was developing a tremendous respect for Curtis and didn't have any doubt in her mind that he could do anything in the world he put his mind to, legs or no legs. It would make a difference if he were really a cripple she thought, but I'd have to think about the children I'll have someday, what kind of life they'd have. I'm not noble, not when it comes to that.

After lunch, they went to a little park that had a beautiful rose garden. They exchanged roses there, smiling at each other. Curtis was still shy, and Bonnie loved it. This is romantic she thought, and she loved that, too.

They went back for one more fitting of Curtis' legs; then they headed for home. Curtis let Bonnie drive the car for awhile, and that was a first for him, trusting a girl that much. As they entered the Craters of the Moon, the sun was just dipping down below the horizon. It was so beautiful, they stopped and watched. It was warm and peaceful there. They got out and explored, poking around the lava cones and caverns and bubbles. They climbed the huge hill of volcanic ash, Curtis in his wheelchair, weaving back and forth across the path. He came back down like he'd been shot out of a cannon, laughing his head off.

When they got back in the car, Curtis felt like he wanted to tell Bonnie that he thought she was terrific, that he'd had more fun with her than he'd had with anybody for a long time. She was making him feel things he never thought he'd feel. But how could he say things like that without making it sound sappy? He didn't know, so his mind began exploring avenues.

He pretended he was calling someone on the phone, and she took his cue. "George?" he asked. "Yes," she answered. He told George about the day and about the girl, how beautiful she was, what he thought of her.

"Okay," she said and made her own phone call and her own disclosures.

Remembering it all later on, when they were each safe at home, they were amazed.

The next Saturday, Bonnie had two dates. In the afternoon, she went with Curtis to Island Park. They spent the time hiking around and taking pictures of each other. Then they had to leave so that Bonnie could have time to get ready for her evening date. Curtis thought it was a horrible bummer, but he was gracious about it, and he got her home in time, even though he was hoping maybe a tire would blow.

That night Bonnie was stood up! It had never happened to her before in her life, and she was so mad she could have smacked somebody. "For this I came home early?" she said. She stormed on over to Curtis, talking the evening away. Finally, he went up to his room, and he didn't come down for a little while, so she thought he was gone for good. She thought it was a little strange that Curtis would leave her like that, no good night or anything, so she let Alan walk her home, feeling horrible inside.

No sooner had she walked through her door when the phone started to ring.

"Hey, Bonnie, why didn't you wait? I was going to walk you home." She really would have felt bad then, if she hadn't felt so pleased. She told Curtis she could always go right back over to his place so he *could* walk her home. He declined the offer, but he told her that he wanted to see her the next day. When she hung up, she pressed her face into her hands, hard, and when she dropped them, she was smiling.

Bonnie and Curtis became an institution. They had a class together, Dr. Lowder's anatomy and physiology, and they competed for grades. They spent a lot of evenings quizzing each other on the phone. Once they had a big exam on Monday, so they each went to their respective beds at six Sunday evening, setting their alarms for midnight so they could spend the rest of the night popping questions at each other over the phone. They both got A's. But that wasn't the only successful result of their studying.

The first real test of their relationship was Brad. Brad was a big, strong, handsome, young man who had been a friend of Curtis' and who had been interested in Bonnie before Curtis had come along. Brad came all the way from Salt Lake City just to see her, so she had to go out with him. It wasn't like she minded going, either; at least, that's the way it seemed to Curtis when she told him about it.

"Fine," he said determinedly. "If she can go out with him, I can play the same game."

So Brad and Bonnie went to the dance, and Curtis and Karen went to the show, both ending up in the Student Union Building. When they passed, as it was inevitable they must, Curtis felt a nice, mean little satisfaction — until he saw Bonnie's face. It was a few days before they could patch it up again.

Time rolled along, and soon it was April, 1974. Things were very good, and the coming of spring was making them even better. Curtis was feeling strong and fit, and he handled the wheelchair like it was part of him. Up to this point Bonnie had been very solicitous of him, helping Curtis up over curbs, sometimes even pushing the chair for him. But as time went on and his independence began to assert itself, the only pushing Bonnie did was to the top of the hill by her dorm, where they performed a little daily ritual on their way to campus. They'd get just to the brink of the hill, then Bonnie would hop on behind Curtis, and the two of them would whoop and holler as they flew down the hill at an incredible rate of speed.

When Curtis heard about the Primary Children's walk-a-thon, he toyed with the thought that he might try it. Every year the Primary Children's Hospital had a fund raising, and this year it was a twenty-one mile walk. The participants had to secure pledges, a certain amount of money for every mile they ended up walking, so the further each person walked the more money he or she personally contributed. Curtis was thinking he would go the entire distance in his wheelchair.

He approached Bonnie with the idea, and she told him that if he would do it, she would, too. She had been quite the star in high school track, and she'd kept herself in shape since then, so she was equal to the challenge.

The next Saturday, Curtis and Bonnie joined over four hundred students who were making the walk. It was really something, all those healthy little people going that distance so unhealthy ones would have a better chance at life. The day was

beautiful, and there was no hurry about the walk; it wasn't a race
— it was more like a test of endurance. For the first little while,
the going was easy and pleasant.

The hours wore on. Curtis' elbows and shoulders were
throbbing, and his arms were getting stiff. He was getting horrible
blisters on his hands where he kept making contact with the
wheels. But Curtis didn't want to stop. He had always enjoyed
doing something like this, something with a start and a finish,
even though it might be hard, and there was something about this
particular chore that made him very determined to go the
distance.

Finally they could see the finish line. They had been on the
road seven and a half hours.

Curtis was stiff and sore, but he was feeling very good. He
alone had earned a quarter of the money that had come in, but
more important, now he knew that his body was capable of far
more than he had been asking from it. He found himself
wondering how far he could push himself, how much he really
could do. He enjoyed the fuss everybody was making over him.
And the pride in Bonnie's face gave him the greatest pleasure. He
started thinking, maybe this could be the start of something. . . .

But the next morning he wasn't thinking that way anymore.
When he finally woke up, all he could move was his eyes, and
that wasn't easy. He was one big sore muscle.

Alan came up and shook him by the shoulder, saying,
"Curtis, come on! Time for priesthood! Rise and shine!" And if
Curtis could have moved at all, he would have flattened Alan.

Instead, he gritted his teeth and said, "I can't move. I'm not
kidding."

So Alan enlisted the help of some of the guys next door, and
as a team, they got Curtis up and dressed him. They stuck him
into his chair and pushed him to church and generally had a great
time of it.

The end of the year came too soon. By that time, Curtis was no longer Curtis. Now that he belonged to Bonnie, he was "Curt," and Curt he would be from that time on.

It wasn't easy for either of them to think about going home for the summer. They were both a little fearful that someone or something might come along and change things between them.

What made it even worse for Bonnie was that, while she would be going back to Ricks in the fall, Curt was transferring down to B.Y.U. where there were more than twenty-five thousand students, and as reports had it, most of them girls. The distance alone was discouraging.

It really was a nice summer for both of them, and no particular waves came along to rock their happy little boat. They called each other, wrote letters back and forth, and they missed each other. Then Curt invited Bonnie to come and visit for a week before school started.

The morning before she left Bonnie was excited and nervous, and — after a brief visit to the local drug store where she had a heavy whiff of the perfume counter — nauseated. The fact that it was her first flight didn't help her stomach any. But finally, there she was, way up over the high, massive ridges of the Rockies, and she didn't even throw up; but then, she didn't eat anything on the plane either. She just kept her mind on Curt. They had both been letting their hair grow all summer, so she tried to figure out what he was going to look like.

Miles away, Curt was so excited, no way could he keep still long enough to do any successful time killing, so he announced that he was going to the airport, and he took off. As he drove down the highway, he tried to remember Bonnie's face. The eyes were easy, so full of life, so gentle, intelligent, and beautiful. Oh, the things she could say with those eyes. He thought that she is one in a million. She makes most girls look so bad. I've never known any girl so quick to understand things, so kind, sensitive, and so wise. . . . He kept driving faster.

Once he got to the airport, he passed the time playing staring games with the people there. It was more amusing than disturbing for him now, having people notice him so much.

The plane landed. Curt waited at the gate, watching the door of the airplane, hoping to see Bonnie before she saw him, wanting to watch her walk down the ramp. She finally did come out, and they greeted each other, both feeling awkward and shy as people do after long separations, unsure of the reception they would get, unsure of their own feelings on the matter. It wasn't long before Curt's infectious grin got things underway, and they were talking like long lost friends, studying each other covertly, getting re-acquainted.

It was the best of weeks. They fished in the riverbottoms and refinished furniture for Curt's mom, but it really didn't matter what they did — it was the feeling that made everything so nice — that new, secret electricity that is young love. Every moment was almost unbearably glorious to them.

It was over way too soon. Bonnie had to be in Rexburg a few days before school started because she was going to be a resident assistant that year and had to go to orientation meetings. She had stayed out every minute of her time and was almost unconsolable until Curt offered to drive her to Rexburg.

"The insurance company I've been selling for has their main office up there," he said. "I was going this week to help them out anyway, so I'll just take you up."

That made the trip very nice, and she thought Curt might be able to stay there for a few days.

When she got to the first meeting, feeling ready for business, she was more than a little surprised to find Curt there, evidently waiting for her.

"And what are you doing here?" she asked him. "I thought you were supposed to be selling insurance."

"Oh, I am," he said, smiling this utterly Cheshire smile at her. "But since I know Wood Miller, your housing coordinator, . . . well, I thought I'd just sit in with you and see what's goin' on these days."

But then, he took notes during the meeting. She'd look at him like, what are you *doing?* And he'd shrug and smile that catty smile. Strange boy, she thought to herself. I wonder what he's up to?

At lunch time, Mr. Miller handed out the meal tickets. Curt got one. Bonnie looked at the ticket, and then she looked at Curt. Then she narrowed her eyes. "Explain *that*, please?" Curt looked her straight in the eye, solemn as a judge with an acquittal up his sleeve.

"I did a very good job for him last year, that's all," he said as they went down to lunch. "He's grateful."

Bonnie seemed to accept Curt's answers, somewhat dubiously, until they passed a table of the residents from Curt's old dorm and were greeted with such suspicious epithets as "Glad to have you back, Curt," and "It'll be a great year with you around again, Brinkman." Even love couldn't defend her trust against assaults like that, and besides, by this time, Curt was laughing his head off.

"Okay, Bozo," she said, stopping dead in the middle of the aisle. "What's going on?" He smiled again and held up a hand, as much as to say, "Okay, you've got me," and he led her to a table. There he explained that he had decided not to transfer to B.Y.U. — because if she was at Ricks, that's where he wanted to be. They were both a little non-plussed by the strength of the statement, but it couldn't have made Bonnie happier.

CHAPTER NINE
The Challenge

The next few days at the college dorm were a bedlam of preparations and beginnings, getting people checked in, taking care of the problems, making sure there were enough sheets, meal tickets, and what not. It was very difficult for Bonnie and Curt to get together, at least at any normal time of the day. So, on the first day of school, they got up at four a.m. and went to Rexburg park, where they built a fire and cooked breakfast over it. It was a quiet, mellow time — almost spiritual — and it seemed wonderful to Bonnie to be so close to someone who could think of doing something like that. It was like something you'd read in a book, a fairy tale or something, all glittering with morning dew and love. It was inevitable that reality would intrude. Eight o'clock came, and it was time to go to class.

But that was only a small thing, a minor interruption. What actually intruded was Curt's fear. He had done a lot of thinking since he'd let Bonnie know he was staying in Rexburg for her, and his thoughts were taking on the line of wait a minute, am I ready for this? He had spent very little time in the society of young women, being shy the way he was. Marriage was for Curt, as it is for most LDS people, a very permanent thing — it excluded the possibility of any other attachments in the future. You chose your wife, and that was it.

He wondered how would he know how to make that kind of choice? What kind of knowledge would he be basing his decision on? He was feeling very much like he had leaped before he'd looked, and it frightened him. He felt he needed to "shop" a little, so his decision could be an intelligent one. He needed more experience. On the other hand, what if Bonnie really was the very best thing in the world, and he lost her because he went around trying to find out if she was the right one?

The upshot of all this thinking was that his behavior around Bonnie became more distant, less comfortable, and she felt the change just as surely as she felt the cold winds bringing winter down from the mountains.

They had a talk. Bonnie was dignified. She listened with her face quietly composed, trying to convince both of them that she wasn't having her legs kicked out from under her. Curt explained to her, carefully, awkwardly, that he needed to go out and see other girls. And at that moment, it all seemed fair. Perhaps not really fair — but Bonnie was leaning over backwards not to seem selfish about the whole thing.

The weeks went by. She tried to be magnanimous, tried not to let this get to her. Then it was Curt's birthday. Surely he will save a special time like this for me, she assured herself mentally. She asked him to dinner but got no answer. So she made him a present and took it to the lab they shared together.

She was quiet about giving him the gift; it was all so unsure — she wasn't walking on steady ground. Neither was Curt. He smiled, but not like he used to, and he took the present. When he unwrapped it, he held the decoupaged plaque in his hands and smiled again, the same unhappy way. Bonnie took a little courage from that.

"Am I going to see you later to celebrate your birthday?" she asked, feeling like she was pretty safe in asking.

Curt looked up sharply. He said, "Ah — no, I've got something I've gotta do."

Then it was Bonnie's turn to smile the sad smile. There didn't seem to be anything anyone could say, really, so they went back to their lab work. The question burned in Bonnie's mind, What do you need to do that's more important than I am? but she didn't ask it; she allowed her unhappiness no voice at all, but her hands shook a little in spite of all that.

Later, home alone, she could no longer contain her frustration. She picked up the phone, feeling uncomfortable with what she was doing, and called Curt's apartment. There was no answer.

She went to bed confused and frightened.

A few days later she still hadn't heard from Curt, and there was a dead weight in her chest. She just didn't understand at all, but she was afraid that she did understand. If a man loves a woman, she couldn't help thinking, he doesn't let days go by without at least calling.

She had to go to the library that day to do some studying, and she ran into Curt there. When she saw him, her misery welled up inside of her, and her pride went away. He said, "Hello," and it was as noncommittal a hello as she'd ever heard.

"Curt, what's going on? Things aren't the same anymore. Where were you on your birthday night?" Bonnie asked inquisitively.

He looked at her, and his jaw tightened a little. He gave it to her straight, "I went to a movie with another girl."

It was like he'd hit her in the face. She chilled all over with embarrassment, then grief. Without a word, she turned around and walked away from him, out of the library. That's when she began to cry. When she got outside and the first little flakes of early winter snow hit her hot cheeks, she started to run. She ran until she couldn't run anymore, working out her outrage and the sudden sense of loss that was making her feel like she was a vacuum inside. Her crying was the kind that came in heavy sobs, and it made it hard for her to breathe.

Inside the library, Curt was still where she had left him. He had justified his birthday night to himself a hundred times, until he had felt just fine about it. The look on Bonnie's face had disturbed him. He had suddenly realized how much the situation had really hurt her. But he was angry inside, too. He felt like it was unfair that he was in a position to hurt her, like he was trapped, and he resented the feeling.

I'm doing what I have to do, he thought to himself, putting a clamp on the urge to follow Bonnie and comfort her. He went back to his books.

The next few days were like a nightmare to Bonnie. Coming to terms with pain isn't easy for anyone. Rationally, she realized that Curt needed this room, this growth. She had dated a lot. She had a lot of experience with people, and he just didn't have that yet. She wanted him to come to her because he had chosen her above all others, not because she was the only one, the easy way out.

The hardest thing was that he wanted her to sit around doing nothing. What if he did find someone he liked better? Where would that leave her? That's when she was no longer rational and would say, "Fine, just eat my dust, buddy." But that feeling never won; she had this very deep conviction that the kind of bond that had formed between the two of them was stronger than this whole mess, and the relationship just wasn't meant to be a passing experience. That's why she couldn't let go.

But she also couldn't demean herself. They had planned that Bonnie would go home with Curt over Thanksgiving. That was obviously not going to be the thing to do, so she went to Denver, and while she was there, he called her, only to say that he definitely needed to date around. This time he released her, saying he thought they ought to call things off. There was a little relief in that. At least she knew where she stood.

The rest of the semester passed quickly. Bonnie did very well in her classes, and Curt did very well in his social development, becoming heavily involved in student government and getting so all-fired popular that his roommate started calling him "Big Man on Campus," BMOC for short.

Two of the women's sororities voted Curt "Guy of the Year" and "Man for All Seasons." He worked in the Ombudsman's office, and everybody knew him. He loved it. He couldn't believe how good it felt to have people look at him, not because he was in a wheelchair, but because he was somebody.

Christmas came and went. The only communication between Curt and Bonnie was a phone call. She still felt that bond between them, but she didn't see how anything could ever become lasting. Curt was for sure going down to the "Y" for winter semester — he had graduated from Ricks just before Christmas. Provo, Utah was a long way away, but not as far away from her as Curt was, himself, at this point.

Bonnie went back to school early after vacation, reconciled to Curt's physical absence. But there he was in Rexburg again, announcing that he had decided to stay that last semester so he could take a few classes he was interested in. Bonnie just couldn't figure him out, but she *did* know that things were going to be rough, "having him around without having him around."

Their relationship really died at the beginning of the semester. Then Curt started coming around again. One night they were driving home from an activity — Curt was very quiet. Without taking his eyes off the road, he said, "What would you think if I told you I thought I loved you?"

Bonnie kind of smiled.

"I'm not trying to tell you we are going to get married," he said. "I don't want to scare you off."

Bonnie looked at him. "I've known for a long time that I love you," she said. And that was all.

The spring came. Bonnie stayed in Rexburg, working in a potato factory and finishing her degree in time for June graduation.

Curt went home to Shelley, where he had a lot of heavy thinking to do. That was when he found out that someone was trying to beat his Primary Children's walk-a-thon record, trying to bring in more money than he had. They didn't succeed, but even the fact that they had tried was bothering Curt. He found out that he really wanted to stay on top of things, that if somebody was going to try and break his record, he was going to go out and do something else, something to blow everybody away.

That's when he conceived his Yellowstone trip. At first, he was just going to do 100 miles somewhere in Idaho, then he thought Yellowstone would be more exciting, and he was going to raise money for something while he went. He organized a committee, getting one of the local Lion's Clubs behind him to help with the organization and promotion, to make arrangements, and to supply an escort so Curt wouldn't be alone if he got hit by a car or something on the way.

He got the Idaho Falls 4-H Club to go around collecting pledges, and he, himself, addressed a number of clubs and lunch groups on the subject, until finally they had enough money pledged to make the thing a significant event.

The news media ate it up, and he was getting terrific coverage. In fact, the day the trip was supposed to start, one of the news stations got to Yellowstone before he did, and they were talking to the rangers, trying to find Curt. That was the first the rangers had heard about the things, and when they got together to talk it over, they decided that a wheelchair trip through the wilds of Yellowstone wasn't a very good idea.

By this time Curt was out about fifteen miles north of the south entrance to the park and was just finishing up his second actual mile when a ranger came up and pulled him off the side of the road to tell him they weren't going to let him wheel in there. He told Curt the whole thing was a safety hazard, both to Curt and to the traffic because the roads were so narrow and winding.

He told the ranger he understood and that he had to wait by the side of the road for his Lion's Club escort, who was off seeing the sights and who was supposed to meet him at a certain point along the way. Curt sat there for two hours before his escort finally came.

Curt told him how the situation was and that he would just start in Teton National Park instead. After wheeling about fifteen miles into Teton Park, it started to get dark, so Curt stopped at a picnic area where he cooked himself a little meal over a fire. Two couples came along and joined him; one of the couples was from Washington, D.C. and the other from Denver. They were young people who were out to see the sights, and they sat there with Curt and chatted till it got quite late.

When they finally left, it was very dark. Because of certain rules about camping in picnic areas, Curt was faced with having to find a place to sleep — somewhere else. There was no way he was going to ride around in his wheelchair in the dark, looking for a place to camp, so he found a little place down just off the road, and that's where he spent the night, hoping the whole time that the rangers wouldn't see him and kick him out.

It was cloudy that night. Curt rolled out his sleeping bag and put his poncho over him as a tent and tried to go to sleep, but he kept worrying, what if it rains on me? What if a bear comes and gets me? Then he finally went to sleep.

Curt woke up at six, ate some breakfast, and started out again. He had his pack on the back of the chair and his sleeping bag on top of that. It was so early that there was no traffic at all, except one ranger who kept driving by. Curt had done about five miles, and he'd just climbed the last mile and a half of it up to the top of a hill when the ranger came up and pulled him off onto a ramp at the side of the road. The ranger said that he'd talked to his supervisor, and they couldn't let Curt wheel along on those roads. He just generally gave Curt the same story they'd given him at Yellowstone.

"Now you stay right here off the road, and I'll go get a pickup or a station wagon so that I can get your chair into the car and down to Coulter Bay to where my headquarters are."

Curt said, "Okay," but very hesitantly. Then the ranger took off. Curt waited a few minutes; then he started to get angry. "This isn't fair," he fumed. He'd just done a mile and a half uphill, and the next two miles down into Coulter Bay were all downhill. "And they want me to sit here after I did all this work? No way; they're not getting away with this." So he took off down the hill.

It was great. The wind was whipping him in the face, and he was really feeling the speed. He'd gone down quite a way when all of a sudden, the ranger was coming back up — all he could do was watch as Curt shot by going down the other way.

There was a side road about a hundred yards further down. Curt scooted off onto the side road, going in about three miles, then just sat there for awhile, being eaten up by mosquitoes. He was spraying the repellant like crazy, but it wasn't doing any good they were so thick. He decided the rangers were going to get him sooner or later anyway, and he couldn't sit there forever, so he went out onto the main road again. He'd gone another hundred yards or so when the ranger came up and pulled off on the other side of the road in the gravel.

The ranger waved for Curt to come on over across to him. Curt shook his head. He signalled again. Curt shouted, "No!" The ranger hollered at him, "You get over here, or I'm going to have to come and get you."

So Curt finally went over to the other side of the road. They were sitting there next to the tail-end of the station wagon the ranger had brought back, having a little discussion as to why Curt didn't think he should have to get in and why he should be able to continue. By this time the morning had bloomed, and there was a lot of traffic.

The discussion got a little hotter and a little more specific — now concerning whether Curt was going to get into the car or not. Finally, the ranger said, "Listen, if I have to use force, I'm going to use force to get you in there."

Curt said, "Okay, let's go," and he put up his fists. He wasn't skinny, and he was thinking he could hold his own. All these cars were going by. Curt couldn't help saying quietly to himself, "Here they are, watching this ranger and this poor little guy in a wheelchair who doesn't have any legs, and the ranger's going to beat up on him; he's got his fists up, and nobody will even stop to help him. This is incredible. It's also ridiculous." Curt looked at the ranger. He's not going to hit me, and we're just going to sit here, and he's going to go on and on, and we're just going to waste a lot of time. So Curt finally crawled into the car.

They drove down to ranger headquarters, and Curt had another run-in with the supervisor. "This is not my fault," Curt kept saying. "I'm not hard to get along with."

The supervisor was worse than any of the others. His big argument was, "The people who come into this park are paying taxes."

Curt said, "I pay as much taxes as anybody else does."

"Well, you're not paying gasoline taxes."

Curt thought this whole thing was unbelievable! The guy had to be a complete idiot. Because he didn't put gasoline in his wheelchair, he didn't pay taxes. It was incredible. He said, "Oh, you mean that you have people come in here, and you don't let them get out of their cars and walk around at all, and you don't let people in on bicycles?" Curt knew better than that — he biked through the park before his accident, and he knew people who did it all the time.

Well, the bottom line of the discussion was that Curt could not, under any circumstances, wheel through the park, so he ended up finishing the trip in Idaho. He just thought that he'd go to his own home state where there are decent people. He went through Island Park and had some very nice experiences. One day he did forty-five miles, another day thirty. He ended up getting the full hundred and twenty miles done in five days, even making up the time he'd lost with the rangers.

It was hard for him to believe that all that bedlam had happened, especially since the rangers knew it was a big fund raising venture for mentally handicapped children.

Curt did the distance without further trouble, and it was the first really long distance trip he'd attempted. There were a lot of reporters there at the end, and the last question they asked Curt was, "What do you want to do next?" That was a good question. At the time, Curt just said that he was going to play basketball. It was a simple enough answer, but there would be a mountain of work behind it. Curt knew now that he could do anything he wanted to, something Bonnie had known from the very beginning.

Another thing he was learning was that it felt good to be remarkable. He'd lost his legs, but he was getting famous. People were saying, "Look at what that kid can do." And he remembered how he had felt in the hospital, that one night when he had felt so hopeful about his life. That night he thought maybe he could help other people. Now he knew he could. "I want them to know what I know," he said to himself. "I know I can do things, and I know I can *keep* doing things."

After that, he could feel a little better about going back to face Bonnie.

CHAPTER TEN
True Love

When the autumn finally rolled around, Bonnie had transferred to B.Y.U. Curt drove her down to Utah a couple of weeks early so she could find a job. Bonnie didn't like it in Provo; she was afraid of being alone, and she didn't know a soul at the "Y." When it came time for Curt to go back to Idaho, Bonnie cried and cried.

"Oh, Curt," she said. "I just want to go back with you."

So he drove her back to Idaho that night, and she stayed with his family one more week. The next trip down was more successful, and Bonnie stayed, but it wasn't easy for her. Curt had decided to stay in Idaho for the fall semester. By this time they had talked about marriage a little; Curt still wasn't too sure about it all.

A few weeks into the term, Curt wrote and asked Bonnie when he should come down to see her. Her answer was, "Wednesday." So when Wednesday came, Curt came with it.

They packed a picnic and headed up Provo Canyon. The canyon was breathtaking that time of year, and the Indian summer afternoon was warm. They went up to Canyon Glen and sat out on the rich green lawn. Every time the wind blew, golden leaves fell around them like rain. This was like magic again, Bonnie thought.

And then Curt started dropping some heavy hints. Maybe he shouldn't come down anymore; it was an awful long trip, and it cost money. Actually, maybe things really weren't going to work out the way they wanted them to. . . .

Why does he always do this to me? she thought. He always

picks the nicest times for the rottenest decisions. It was obvious to her that Curt was trying to tell her it just wasn't going to work for them. He wants out, she thought. What a great way to totally desecrate a nice afternoon. Well, at least it was a decision. They had been tentative for so long she was nearly weary of it.

They drove back down into Provo. Bonnie wasn't particularly talkative. They stopped at the A & W. While sitting there, waiting for their root beer to come, Curt asked Bonnie to get something out of the jockybox.

"It's locked," she said, and that only made her feel funnier — he never kept the glove compartment locked. Everything was so strange. She was just beginning to want to go home and forget the whole thing.

"Oh, never mind," he said, evidently not noticing that anything at all was wrong. "I'll get it later."

That night they went to see "The Other Side of the Mountain." If she had been sad before the movie, she was desolate after it. It was nice, though, to have a legitimate reason to cry a little — even happy people cried when they went to that show. Besides, it was all too close to home.

She couldn't help but feel that Curt was building up to this big, depressing climax. He's going to let me go, and he's never going to see me again, she kept thinking. Bonnie spent the whole evening waiting for the final blow.

They drove around for awhile, looking at Provo, ending way up in the foothills by the LDS temple. Curt parked the car on the road above the temple and leaned back in the seat. "This is the prettiest view in Provo," he said. And the best place for a heavy talk, Bonnie thought.

They talked some, saying nothing in particular, and when Bonnie was about ready to scream, get it over with, can't you? Curt leaned over her and unlocked the glove box.

"Oh, I have something for you," he said.

Terrific, she thought. This is finally it. And he got me a going-away present.

He handed her a little box. She opened it slowly, waiting for the big confrontation. But when she lifted the lid back, a shower of tiny lights played across her face. "Curt," she said, and she lifted the ring with its shimmering stone high out of the box, holding it up against the temple lights.

She looked at Curt, and he was smiling. "I was wondering if you would marry me," he said.

She looked down at the ring again, and she couldn't believe what was happening. A whole new kind of joy was filling her, and when she looked at Curt, it spilled right out of her eyes.

Later, she explained to him what she'd been thinking all day, and they both had a good laugh. They decided they would be married in December. No more magic, Bonnie thought. Now it's real.

The next day Curt and Bonnie drove up to Idaho to tell Curt's parents what had happened. It was a little harder to tell them than Curt had anticipated — he was awfully embarrassed. He beat around the bush for awhile; they couldn't guess why he was uncomfortable. Finally, he said, "I brought Bonnie up here for a reason."

"Oh? What was that?" his dad said, his eyes laughing.

"Can't you guess?" Curt said, almost exasperated. His parents' grins were wide with satisfaction. After two and a half years of courting, it was finally going to happen. The family was thrilled.

The next hurdle was in Bountiful, Utah, where Bonnie's parents were staying for her brother's wedding. When they walked into her Aunt Lucille's living room, they found the entire family there, visiting and talking, and Curt's old shyness reasserted itself. He could barely make friendly conversation, much less an announcement.

Bonnie became impatient and blurted out, "Curt has something to tell you."

Bonnie's parents turned to him, their eyebrows raised. Curt could have wheeled another five hundred miles in that minute and felt better than he felt sitting still under that gaze. He smiled at them a trifle weakly, and he said, "Well, I have this situation that's developed. I'm going to be leaving home, and I need someone to do my ironing and washing and to keep house for me and things."

It was supposed to be funny and lighten things up a little bit. He was trying to ease into the announcement, but Bonnie's folks weren't prepared like Curt's parents had been, and they misinterpreted what he was saying. They saw this young man in a wheelchair, and all they understood was that he needed a maid or a housekeeper to take care of him because he was an invalid. They weren't enthusiastic. Things were off to a bad start.

Bonnie's folks didn't know Curt at all; her mother had met him once, but that was the extent of the acquaintance. As the evening went on, they got to know him better, and they finally understood what he had been trying to say — and why it had come out the way it had. They still weren't happy with the engagement.

They knew that marriage was a difficult thing, even under the best of conditions, and they could foresee problems connected with Curt's disability. They knew Curt and Bonnie were too young and too hopeful to see these problems.

Mr. Hymas asked them to wait at least till spring. He told them that it would be the third wedding in the family in the last year and that financially it would be very difficult. But Bonnie and Curt had very strong feelings about the situation. They would handle the problems, and they would be married in December. In the face of their gentle conviction, Mr. Hymas said he would adjust. What he and his wife would have a very hard time adjusting to was Curt's disability. They didn't understand it, and it made them uncomfortable. They were a little frightened about Bonnie's future with Curt, dubious about its chances for success.

It was only a matter of time, however, before they came to see things differently. They only had to get to know Curt, to see the way he could handle himself, before they began to consider his condition the way he did, *as more of an inconvenience than a disability.* They grew more comfortable with him, and as they did, their support became more wholehearted.

The relationship between the two young people, now free of the games of courtship, grew and flourished like a hardy winter rose, and when the third week in December rolled around, they were ready for their commitment.

Bonnie tried on her wedding dress the day before the wedding. It fit beautifully, a great compliment to her mother. Everything was working out as planned.

The morning of December twentieth dawned soft and pink, warm as spring, and the Idaho Falls Temple gleamed against the blue December sky like a beacon of purity and hope. Curt was at peace. The love he was feeling was strong and unquestionable. Bonnie was a little less confident, being slightly shaken by the preparations and the confusion, normal for this type of occasion. But once she entered the peaceful, quiet temple, her tensions left her, and she, too, felt the pure light of her love, glowing against any darkness, easing any doubts. The question of children never bothered her; her faith whispered to her that all was well, and so her heart was calm.

The room was full of the people they loved best. They knelt across from each other, a beautiful marble altar between them. Curt looked at his sweet bride, and he saw her suddenly for what she was: virtuous, lovely, alive, and warm, and the whiteness around her made Bonnie seem somehow translucent. He could see himself in the mirror behind her, and then again and again as the reflections of the mirror seemed to extend into eternity, as would the covenant they were making.

It was a glad day. Curt and Bonnie were married. It was only the beginning.

CHAPTER ELEVEN
Beginnings: Marriage & Athletics

The first big step in Curt and Bonnie's life together was the move to Provo, Utah, where Curt was going to study psychology at B.Y.U. Because of tight finances, they found a nice, unfurnished apartment and slept in sleeping bags on the floor.

Their love began to grow for each other. Bonnie's folks had been right about one thing — marriage meant doing a lot of adjusting. "You'd think after knowing a person for two years, you'd *know* him," Bonnie would say to herself. There were a lot of things Bonnie was learning about Curt that she'd never known before, and there were a lot of things Curt was learning about Bonnie that were real surprises. They were working hard at adjustment, something Curt already knew a lot about. In other words, they had a very normal, very good marriage going.

One of the things Curt had discovered about Bonnie right away was that cooking wasn't her strong point. Not yet, anyway. One of the things she learned about him was that he was very funny about meeting other people in wheelchairs.

Curtis had seen quite a few wheelchair people on campus and just didn't want to have anything to do with them. It was as if other people were thinking that if there were two guys in wheelchairs, they should get along very well. This implied that the wheelchair was all you needed to have in common with someone, all you needed in order to be great friends. He resented it.

Curt had seen Mike Johnson around, but he hadn't been at all inclined to work up any kind of relationship with him. On the other hand, Mike was very interested in Curt. Mike was a Viet

Nam veteran who had lost his legs and part of his hands to a land mine. It had been a long road back for Mike, but he'd made it, and now he was very much into athletics — the kind that people like Curt Brinkman could do.

Mike was organizing a wheelchair basketball team. It wasn't a new idea; there were already teams that were competing with each other all over the country, but there was no Utah team yet. So Mike was on the lookout for talent, and when he saw the way Curt handled his chair early one morning when Curt was late for class, Mike couldn't resist putting a note on Curt's windshield, inviting him to be part of the team.

Of course, when Curt came back to the car and saw the little piece of paper flapping around in the wind, he just knew it was a security ticket and was upset at whatever officer had neglected to notice his handicap sticker. He was greatly relieved to find that he'd been mistaken, but then he was troubled by the contents of the note. He wasn't at all sure how he felt about the whole thing and for awhile, at least, chose to ignore the invitation.

Meanwhile, Mike worked on Bonnie. One day Bonnie had been waiting for Curt to get out of class, and Mike drove up. He talked to Bonnie for awhile, asking if she were Curt's wife or girlfriend. He left her with a nice feeling. She did the best she could to communicate that feeling to Curt, and finally he did join the team.

It was a good decision. In fact, it was to be one of the major directional decisions of his life, although it seemed a simple thing then. The most important part of his experience with wheelchair basketball was that he really enjoyed it. The competition was great.

Bonnie went with him to the games, watching him have a good time, watching him grow stronger. The first game she went to caused her to nearly fall right off the bleachers at halftime when some of the players just got up out of their wheelchairs and walked away. She'd been thinking that all the players were like Curt, permanently disabled, and she couldn't understand why no one else in the place was reacting to this tremendous miracle that had just happened. She learned right away that people with even small disabilities could play.

As the season progressed, Curt fell in love with athletics all over again. He became good friends with Mike, and that relationship soon included wives as well. It turned out that Mike and his wife, Jan, had been married one day before Curt and Bonnie, and since they'd had some of the same adjustments to make, the two couples could base their friendship on a good degree of understanding.

Toward the end of the season, the Utah team played Colorado, and Curt — now a real contender — ended up colliding a couple of times with Jerry Deets of the Colorado team. After the game, Jerry sought Curt out, telling him that he might really be able to do something with his speed *if* he could learn to control his chair. He told Curt all about the organized para-track and field that was going on, and he got Curt so excited that the next day Curt sent for the necessary papers from the regional office. Curt leaped into wheelchair track and field, pulling Mike along with him.

Curt initiated wheelchair track and field in Utah. During the first year, he did very well — well enough that even Bonnie was surprised. It seemed that he had a natural talent for track and had a strong body. The competition made him even stronger, giving him the motivation he needed to keep himself in shape. Curt excelled, and he loved it.

Curt and Mike wanted to do well in the San Jose regionals. They trained their hearts out, wheeling the backroads until they thought their arms would fall off, weight lifting in the Nautilus gym at the "Y," getting in every minute of practice and training they could. So far it had paid off, and their bodies were more than ready. There was only one hitch — money.

Wheelchair athletes are self-supporting, paying their own way to competition. Curt and Mike didn't have the money to get to Salt Lake City, let alone San Jose, California. They needed a sponsor and looked for one almost as hard as they had trained, but it was all to no avail. They couldn't find anyone willing to help them go.

Just a few days before they were supposed to leave, someone told the two that the kids at Scera Park Elementary School in Orem had heard about their problem and were determined to raise the money the athletes needed. The kids really scrambled; mowing lawns, shining shoes, selling anything and everything, and they raised $1,193.43! They invited other schools to help and collected another $290.00.

A few hours before they were to leave, Curt and Mike were introduced to the children at the school, where they staged a hot wheelchair exhibition that was given a standing ovation. Then the children presented the Wheelers with their money.

After the ceremony was over, the kids came up for autographs, and it was almost more than the two young men could take. Curt later talked about it, "I have never seen anything like this. It's one of the most touching things I've ever seen. To see the work the kids put in this means more than anything." Mike said simply, "Knowing the kids are behind us means so much more."

Curt and Mike were the first Utahns ever to enter either regional or national competition. More importantly, they carried the hopes and faith of hundreds of very young people with them. They weren't sure how they'd measure up when they met the kind of guys who were used to this competition, but they did know one thing — they were going to give it their best shot.

The regionals turned out to be a lot more comfortable than Curt had expected. He met some good people there, many talented athletes. The competition was tough, and the boys from Utah really weren't prepared; they just didn't have enough experience yet. Their chairs were too heavy; most of the athletes had lightweight, trim chairs that handled like air. Curt and Mike hadn't raced enough to know the tricks. But they kept their eyes open and learned.

The Utah Wheelers weren't the stars of that meet, but they won enough points to make the Western team and to compete in the nationals at New York City in mid-July.

Money was the problem again. It cost a good amount to get four people — the wives would not be left behind for anything — from Utah to New York. They planned the trip very carefully, and they all got right to work so that by the time July rolled around, they had enough money to make the trip in style. They left a week early and stayed at the Hilton, right in the middle of Manhattan.

Curt didn't want to leave the hotel room. Bonnie kept saying, "This may be our only chance *ever* to see New York," until she finally got him into the elevator and out on the street. They rented a car and spent a few days playing tourists, going up to the top of the Empire State Building, taking in Fifth Avenue, and Time Square. They went to the Waldorf Astoria and saw the singing group the "Fifth Dimension," and they established a favorite watering hole, Mama Leones, an Italian restaurant.

Curt had a classic case of "The Idaho Boy Meets the Big City," being amazed at some of the colorful, not to say strange, characters indiginous to that area of the country. One person they saw was sitting in the gutter playing the curb with a couple of sticks like he was doing a drum solo.

The traffic was another thing that had Curt feeling a little out of his element. At first he was so careful with that rented car, but driving defensively in New York meant sitting still while everyone else whipped around you. Curt became so tired of creeping along that soon he was driving like a native, weaving in and out of the traffic like a crazy person, enjoying every frightening minute of it. Miraculously, there were no accidents.

When the young Wheelers finally competed, they did fairly well — Mike wheeling away with two gold and Curt with two bronze medals. The two did well enough that they made the U.S. team for the 1976 Para-Olympiad that was to be held in Toronto a short time later.

It was in Toronto that Curt set a world record for the hundred meter dash: nineteen and seven-tenths seconds. He also took some bronze medals, one in the discus, one in lawn bowling, a very genteel European sport, and one in shot put. That's not too bad for a beginner!

In the course of those two weeks in Canada, Curt met Bobbie Hall, the father of wheelchair marathons and the first Wheeler ever to run in the Boston Marathon. His excitement about marathoning was infectious, so when Curt got home from Toronto, there were two goals he just had to reach: make the U.S. team for the 1980 Olympics and win the Boston Marathon.

Bonnie had stayed home from the Olympic trip, and it had been a long two weeks for her. She had finished five baby afghans the first week, even though there were no babies in sight yet, and she was more than ready to hear all about Curt's trip. He told her about the political hassles they'd had with the South African and Cuban teams, and he told her how he'd read in a Toronto paper that Moscow — where the 1980 Olympics would be held — would not have anything to do with the Para-Olympiad. "They say there are no disabled in Russia," Curt told her, shaking his head.

"Too bad for them," she said. "They don't know what they're missing."

The following April, 1977, was Curt's first Boston Marathon. As always, money was a problem, but somehow everything was taken care of, and Curt finished second, coming in only three minutes behind Bob Hall, the man who had talked him into running the race. Curt came in at two hours, forty-three minutes and twenty-five seconds; Hall's record was two hours forty minutes.

It was a good beginning to an exciting year for Curt. He and Bonnie had just found out that Bonnie was pregnant, something that they had hoped for ever since the beginning, and the relief and joy Curt got out of that discovery pushed him to great accomplishment.

In May he was awarded the Golden Key Award by Utah Governor, Scott Matheson. In July he won the Salt Lake Deseret News Marathon in the wheelchair division. The U.S. Jaycees selected him as one of the Outstanding Young Men of America, and he and Mike planned a record-breaking tour around Utah Lake.

The Utah Lake trip was going to be a hard one. It was one hundred fifteen miles. The furthest Curt had ever done was forty-five miles, and Mike's big record was twenty-six. It was late August when they started the trip, and Bonnie and Jan followed them in a van all the way. Bonnie was eight months pregnant then, with swollen ankles and every other problem typical of someone in that stage of development. Riding in the van was almost too much work for her.

Ostensibly, Curt and Mike were going the distance so that they could raise the four thousand dollars Utah County needed to purchase a van for servicing the handicapped folks in the area. Of course, there was a lot more to it than that. Curt loved a tough challenge, and he had a fair appreciation of the attention he received when he succeeded. Mike later stated, "It was kind of more of a challenge for me than it was specifically to help someone else, to see if I *could* go around the lake, if I *could* finish."

They started at K-96 Radio in Provo in the early hours of the morning. Hours later, when they reached the little village of Palmyra, they were met by a Mormon bishop and his family who presented them with the money his ward had raised. Just before they got to Genoa, they came across a young rattlesnake that kept trying to kill the wheelchairs by striking at the wheels.

The young Wheelers were raced by calves and bawled out by belligerent chattering gophers. By the time the sun had climbed into a scorching position, they had done all of thirty miles.

At Genda Curt and Mike ate lunch and talked to TV reporters, then they headed out towards Goshen. It was empty, desolate country they were passing through, and the going was hot, long, and beginning to be painful. Just when Curt and Mike thought they might die of boredom, not to mention heat exhaustion, the traffic began to pick up a little.

A Porsche came roaring up behind the van, as though the driver couldn't see the road ahead. He didn't even acknowledge the van until he was right on top of it. By that time there was no time to brake, so the Porsche veered out into the other lane and shot down into the barrow pit until it got around the van. When it came up out of the ditch, raising dust, it nearly collided with Mike. The driver finally pulled out of the plunge and whizzed by Curt, never stopping to apologize for having given Mike a near cardiac arrest.

The two Wheelers decided they preferred boredom to that kind of excitement. They had done about fifty miles by then, and their wrists were starting to complain. A group of kids came out and followed them for awhile on bikes, asking questions and yelling. The company took the young men's minds off their discomfort, but when the kids finally left them, the pain was still there.

They stopped for a rest and a salt tablet, and everyone in the van started telling them they had done enough. "Come on, Mike," Jan said. "Fifty miles left and look at you. Nobody will blame you if you quit now. Look what you've done already!"

They kept going. The west side of the lake seemed all uphill, and the wind was blowing against them. The sun beat down just like it does in all the desert movies, and just when they thought maybe they weren't going to make it, the rain came. It made the rims wet, which was uncomfortable, but the rain was so cool and such a break from the glaring sun, it gave them new life.

As the Wheelers approached Lehi, they were joined by a group of joggers. After that, more and more people joined in, so that by the time they wheeled by the Geneva Steel Plant, there was a huge crowd of people waving, honking, and cheering. Even so, those last few miles were an agony.

Curt's hands, arms, and buttocks were numb, and he was getting awful pains in his back. "My lower back was just killing me from pushing forward and coming down and back up and down, then back up," he said later. "I was so stiff and sore that I couldn't sit up straight. It was incredible. The part that got me the worst was in the wrists and fingers. They are not built to work like ankles and feet, so the tendons and muscles were really overworked. It just wiped me out royal!"

Mike also described the trauma of those last few miles. "I wasn't so sure that I could really finish. The last stretch was agony — it was horrible. I was so sore from bending over, leaning over, and pushing my chair through the rain and wind that my back just about fused in one position. I would then look up and try to straighten my back and scream from the pain. The pain was so intense I would almost pass out. Then I would bend over, push three or four more times, try to sit up and straighten my back, and yell. Then I would go down and push three or four more times, coast and sit up, and yell. That Geneva road seemed so long. Jan was crying and begging me to quit, but something in me wouldn't do that."

And quit they didn't. At approximately 11:00 p.m. in darkness made into dusk by the headlights of many cars, two wheelchairs with their completely fatigued and pain-racked occupants rolled across the finish line. They had done it, covering one hundred fifteen miles in sixteen hours! The world record up to that point had been one hundred and eight miles in five days. When they finally pulled into the boat harbor, Bonnie and Jan were playing the theme from "Rocky" over the van's loudspeaker. It wasn't the last time in his life that Curt would identify strongly with the music from that film.

That fall Curt and Mike were the first students ever invited to light the "Y" for B.Y.U. at a football game. It was a tremendous honor. Unfortunately, Curt and Bonnie's baby was due the day before homecoming, so Bonnie was reasonably sure she would have to miss it all. Sure enough, that's what happened.

The baby was breech, so Bonnie's doctor scheduled her for a Caesarean Section on September 27. Bonnie had a tough time in the hospital while she was waiting for the surgery, but the actual operation only took nine minutes. When little Greg was finally born, he didn't cry but just looked around at his new world. Bonnie and Curt were thrilled to have a son. Curt, a typical new father, was terrified to hold the baby. A nurse put a surgical gown and mask on the new dad, who held out his arms like he was going to carry firewood. Little Greg was placed on top of those stiff arms.

The second day Bonnie was in the hospital with Greg, Curt and Mike had the honors of lighting the "Y" on the mountain. Bonnie listened to the proceedings on the radio, wanting so much to be there. The commentator announced all the things Curt and Mike had accomplished, and the last thing he said was, "Curt and his wife are expecting a baby."

"They don't even know it's a boy," Bonnie smiled.

When they brought Greg home, Curt felt a lot more comfortable with him. He sat in the rocking chair upstairs in the nursery and held Greg for five hours while the little one slept. Curt never moved the whole time. He just watched his tiny son and played with the little fingers. It was the beginning of a wonderful new love.

The next April (1978) brought another Boston Marathon. Curt had a new chair that year, and he was feeling prepared. There was a newcomer, a real contender, George Murray, who had set a marathon record in Florida, so the pressure was on.

George Murray turned out to be a real powerhouse. Bonnie listened to the race progress over the walkie-talkies in the wheelchair athlete's bus. The year before she had ridden to the finish line with some of the athlete's wives, and they'd been so late she'd missed seeing Curt come in. This year she determined that things would be different, so she rode to the starting line on the bus with the athletes and then stayed with the bus as it drove to the finish line.

George Murray was first all the way, but Curt was always close behind him. There were hundreds of thousands of people at the race that year, and it seemed to Bonnie that they were all between her and the finish line. The crowd kept pushing her back further and further, but she did see George Murray as he crossed the finish line first, and then she saw Curt.

She was so excited, she pushed her way up through the crowd and broke past the barriers. A policeman grabbed her arm, but she shook free, and she chased Curt down the little alleyway that led under the Prudential Building where the athletes received their after-race medical attention.

She came up behind him, grabbed the back of the chair, and started pushing him. He didn't even know she was there until she got brave and gave him a big kiss. She hugged him just before they passed out of sight, and the crowd cheered. "Unless you are there you just can't imagine what it's like to have five hundred thousand people cheering for one thing. It's just amazing," Bonnie later recalled.

When she finally wheeled Curt down under the building, he broke down, sobbing. It scared Bonnie. She couldn't get anything out of him; she was trying to figure out if he was all right or if he needed a doctor.

He was just totally exhausted. He had given every single, solitary thing he had to that race. Bonnie later related: "I don't think many people ever experience something like that — where you give totally — absolutely everything you have, and there's nothing left in reserve, absolutely nothing left. That's the way Curt was, so exhausted he broke down and wept — he couldn't even talk and tell me what was the matter."

Taking second place again was a little disappointing, but Curt had done his best; at least he couldn't regret later on that he hadn't tried harder. George Murray had set a new record: two hours twenty-six minutes. Curt would work very hard in the future to break that record.

Curt graduated from B.Y.U. that April with a Bachelor's of Science degree in psychology. Then he planned a new event; he was going to wheel from Salt Lake City to Cedar City, a matter of two hundred seventy-five miles, in five days. He was trying to raise twenty-five thousand dollars for Easter Seals. In the end, he only raised twelve thousand, but he had made the trip and set a record, and all in all it was a good experience.

He went to New York for the running of the 1978 New York Marathon, but that turned out to be a nightmare mass of legal problems. The president of the New York Roadrunner's Club, Fred LeBeau, was really against wheelchair runners, and he tried to get a court injunction against Curt and Bobbie Hall so that they couldn't participate. The mayor decided that the race was open to anyone who wanted to run, so Curt and Bobbie did compete, and Curt took first place.

Curt was doing well in marathon competition. He was voted the Most Outstanding Athlete at the Denver Rocky Mountain Regional, and the media kept close track of him. He was determined to win the Boston Marathon in 1979.

In February of 1979, the Brinkman's second baby was born. By then Curt's accident was so far in the past, they had almost forgotten how worried everyone had been about Curt ever being a father. The birth of this baby was again a tremendous joy to Curt and Bonnie.

It was another C-section, a very difficult one. The baby was wedged deep underneath the pelvic bone, and they had to use forceps to get her out, something that is unheard of in Caesaerean surgery. The delivery took forty-five minutes, and Bonnie's recovery was hard, but the baby, Lorian, was healthy, and Curt had his first daughter.

Bonnie was still recovering when the Boston Marathon came around, so she stayed home. That was just as well; it was a very bad year. George Murray was the favorite again, but that wasn't a problem. What made the year a bad one was the weather, a steady drizzle of icy cold rain. It made the rims slippery, so the athletes were having a hard time getting any kind of hold on the wheels to get a decent push.

Curt was the only racer without rubber-coated rims on his wheels. His chrome rims not only made it harder to get a grip, they also conducted the cold from the slush on the streets to Curt's hands, and before too long, his fingers began to hurt.

He remembered one morning when he was thirteen years old, moving pipe; his fingers had hurt like this, and he'd taken off one of his gloves to take a look at them. One of his fingers had turned blue because his circulation wasn't good. He could feel the same thing happening now, and he was only thirteen miles into the race.

"I've already lost my legs," he thought to himself. "I don't want to lose my fingers, too." Curt was in third position at that time, but he pulled off the course. He asked a policeman to find him a way back to the finish line, so the policeman called an ambulance.

While he was waiting for the ambulance, Curt sat on the sideline in the drizzling rain, feeling pretty dismal and worried about the frostbite. A paramedic came and began to work on Curt's fingers, trying to get the circulation going, and while they were sitting there, Curt, disheartened, watched the other racers pass. Bob Hall came by, giving Curt the kind of sympathetic look born of mutual suffering.

The ambulance finally arrived. By that time, the paramedic had made Curt's fingers feel better, and Curt was thinking he should at least try to finish the race. He left the confused ambulance attendants, wheeled back onto the course, and started to push. When he finally got to Heartbreak Hill, he saw Bob sitting off the side. The course was so difficult that day, five of the wheelchair racers were hospitalized for hypothermia. Only a few of the competitors would finish, and they were treated immediately after the race for the same problem.

Bob offered Curt a ride to the finish. "I've got a friend coming to get me," he said.

Curt waved. "Thanks," he yelled. "I'm going to finish."

When he crossed the finish line, he was seventh. It had been a difficult day. "I'll win in '80," he said.

It was later in the year, and Curt had gone to a race in Blooming, West Virginia. They had done a urinalysis study on all of the participants there to check protein, sugar, etc. It wasn't until a week after Curt had come home that the call came.

Bonnie answered the phone. Curt could tell by the look on her face that something was wrong. As she hung up the phone, she had to fight down a fear that was starting to make her feel cold, and she told Curt that the tests had found sugar in his urine. He had diabetes and needed to see a doctor right away!

Curt lived in dreaded fear of the doctor's visit, but finally went to see Dr. Moody who gave him a Glucose tolerance test that took six hours to administer. Dr. Moody tried putting Curt on a diet to see if that would help, but it didn't, so the last week in September, Curt entered the hospital.

He spent five days in the hospital, struggling to become regulated on insulin. He had to take injections every morning, and he had reactions to some of the drugs given him the first few days. At first, Curt was worried about training, about racing, but Dr. Moody assured him that exercise was the best thing for him and encouraged him to keep his training going.

Bonnie had been badly frightened by the whole ordeal. She had always been the strength and faith of the family, sure that Curt could overcome anything, but this was almost too much, and now she was unsure of everything, especially of herself. She was afraid to have Curt come home from the hospital because she was fearful she would feed him wrong or hurt him in some way. She was afraid that it was the end of things, that Curt might never recover sufficiently to be able to keep doing the things he loved so much.

She really should have known better.

CHAPTER TWELVE
The Brutal Boston

Curt sat in the living room by himself, looking out the window at the steel-gray, blistery, January morning. The year, 1980, had just begun. A chill shook him slightly, so he slipped on his pullover, shoved his hands into the pockets, and sank back into the softness of the couch. He knew he should leave soon and wheel out into the cold winter morning — and the Boston Marathon just wasn't that many weeks away — but for now, he allowed himself the luxury of sitting and thinking.

Curt remembered the other Bostons, his seventh place finish, and his two second places in '77 and '78. They really had been victories of a sort. It wasn't *bad* to be second, but it was nothing like coming in first. He *had* to win, just one time. Last year — another chill went through him as he thought about the rain and cold, his frozen fingers — he was lucky to have finished seventh. He remembered the vow he'd made, that he would come back in 1980 and win. So much had happened since then.

The discovery of his diabetes had been a huge shock. They had it under control now, but it meant daily insulin shots that had seriously complicated regular training. Then bursitis in his right elbow had flared up, and it was difficult and extremely painful to push the wheel. At first, the doctor had given him a steroid shot and almost immediately his whole arm had swelled up from wrist to bicept. After that there were weeks of medication, heat packs, whirlpool treatments, hot and cold packs, ultra-sound, and therapy by B.Y.U.'s athletic trainer. Nothing seemed to work. They had even tried a cayenne pepper treatment that one of his neighbors had come up with. Finally, Dr. Brent Pratley, a former physician to the L.A. Rams, put Curt on a strong antibiotic treatment. The elbow cleared up.

So Curt was finally able to begin training on January 1. He started with two mile jaunts, then he went four miles. Even so, after the last few months, his training schedule had been shot to pieces, and whether or not he had time to get into shape before Boston was anybody's guess.

Curt thought about the other Wheelers he would be competing against. George Murray, the record holder, was the favorite, and his time, two hours twenty-six minutes, would be awfully tough to beat. Bob Hall was still regarded as one of the best. Phil Carpenter was strong. So was Martinsen of Washington State. As he thought about the odds, Curt speculated that he might finish fifth or sixth, if he really worked at it.

The 1979 Deseret News Marathon was the race he had used in qualifying for Boston, and it was the slowest wheelchair time anybody had turned in. So no one expected a whole lot from him. No one had looked at Curt closely at all. Curt thought of his heavy old E & J chair — it was the heaviest one of all the competitors' chairs. Everyone else he knew about had built chairs out of lightweight aluminum and chrome alloy.

Curt looked out through the window. It looked like the wind was dying down some. It was time to go work out; four miles today, maybe five tomorrow. He would just have to do the best he could and feel good about whatever happened. When he got out into the winter morning, the sharpness of the air took away his breath and made his blood jump. The smooth, liquid motion of his arms propelled him down the road into the hazy mist the steel plant was spreading across the valley. He sped through the four miles, grunting and straining up the hills, shielding his face from the biting cold with his gloved hand as he coasted down the other side. Finally he did the sprint home where Bonnie, Greg, and Lorian were up and waiting with a hot breakfast. Bonnie's cooking was good now. After breakfast, he showered, shaved, and left for work at Handicapped Awareness.

Each morning was the same, except he kept increasing his

distance toward one hundred miles in a week. Curt also began swimming again. He increased his swim to one mile a day, three times a week. He was feeling more strength in his upper torso and his arms, and he could feel his lungs stretching — his wind was getting a lot better. He thought of Bob Clark, his swimming coach, and the old Ammon pool in Idaho, and he felt grateful. The swimming was really helping.

January went by fairly smooth, but when February rolled around, there was another hitch. Curt had a difference of opinion with his supervisor at Handicapped Awareness, and suddenly he was out hunting the job market. It was frightening, but he and Bonnie exercised their faith, and soon Curt was working again, this time as a comptroller with the Orem Recreation Center. Part of the blessing was that now he had flexible hours and time in the day to train.

By March 1, Curt was training harder than he ever had. He felt good; he felt strong, but he still didn't think he was in the kind of shape he needed to be in to compete with Murray and Hall. He had missed out on too many weeks of training. Curt had heard that his competitors were doing 120 miles a week plus weight training. Some of the racers, the Viet Nam veterans, had disability pensions, so they could put their whole time into training. It was one of the first times in his life he really felt handicapped.

Finally, it came time for Curt and Bonnie to make the big trip. Money, as always, was still a problem, but with Curt's annuity money from Handicapped Awareness and some help from the Kiwanis, Curt and Bonnie deposited their two children in Idaho and flew to Boston. The trip to Boston was very relaxed for Curt. In fact, he was so relaxed Bonnie was amazed. As they talked about it, they decided it was because there was no pressure from anybody else; no one expected him to win, so Curt wasn't worried about running. He was just going to do his best.

Curt and Bonnie got to Boston two days before the race and checked into the Sheraton Hotel. They travelled around the city and met a lot of old friends, among them Hugh and Dottie

Stobbs, from Wheeling, West Virginia, the folks who had discovered Curt's diabetes.

That Saturday morning, the Brinkmans, the Stobbs, and Kim Butler, another good friend, decided to go for a short run to loosen up. Runners in Boston were no novelty, so the little group was largely ignored as they jogged down the old Boston roads. At first the run was fun, but as the miles wore on and the group decided to head back, they realized they were lost. They did finally find their way back, but only after they had gone twice as far as they had planned to go. Bonnie wasn't used to running that kind of distance, and she was tired out, so Curt and Bonnie went to the jacuzzi to soak Bonnie's tired legs. It felt so good to sit in that hot, seething cauldron. A big black man came in and plunged himself down right between Curt and Bonnie. He looked like he was probably somebody important, and Curt was just thinking that he was probably a baseball player when somebody yelled, "Hey, Julius, this hot enough for you?" Suddenly Curt recognized the huge man — it was Julius Irving, the basketball star!

That night Curt and Bonnie watched the movie *Rocky II* on the hotel's closed circuit T.V. The movie was excellent entertainment, but it was even more than that to Curt. He had been thinking of himself as the underdog, just like Rocky Balboa, and he began to feel the Rocky spirit filling him up. It was powerful, the theme song ringing in his brain, and Curt began to believe in himself. Why *couldn't* he win? He had the strength, the ability, the desire. Fifth or sixth place wasn't good enough. He was going to go for it, the big prize. No one ever remembered who got second; second was nothing. Curt Brinkman had paid his dues; it was his year.

The next day they went sight seeing. The big, historic city was fascinating to the young Westerners.

They were riding a bus around town and were talking about their kids. They had been concerned about how Greg would take it when he got old enough to realize that his daddy didn't have any legs. Bonnie had taught Greg all of the parts of the leg, then she'd ask him to point out the parts on her leg. One day, after she'd taught him about the heel, she'd said, "Where's Daddy's heel?"

Greg looked at his dad, then he said, "Daddy doesn't have any feet." It was the first time he had acknowledged the difference in his dad. Bonnie took that opportunity to tell Greg all about the accident, and he seemed to accept it all quite well.

"I hope it won't cause him any difficulties later on," Bonnie commented to her husband.

Curt smiled and shook his head, "We're blessed with extra special kids. Don't you worry about it." He closed his eyes and leaned his head back against the seat, and Bonnie smiled at him before she went back to the magazine she'd been reading.

Before long, there were tears in her eyes, and she gently nudged her dozing husband. "Hey, Curt," she said, "Listen to this story. . . ."

It was about a boy in a foot race. The boy's dad was in the crowd, watching his son. The boy wanted so badly to impress his dad, to win the race for his dad. The starting gun exploded, and the runners were off. The boy ran so hard he lost his balance and fell. He was sick; no way could he win after that. He looked up, and his dad caught his eye. The dad's eyes said, "Get up, run, you can do it!"

The boy got up and sprinted after the rest of the boys. He began to catch up — he drew even with the back runners — then down he went again. Once more the embarrassed son looked up and got his dad's message, and once more he got up and ran. He was working so hard to catch up, and he was so desperate to please his dad that he tripped all over himself and fell for the third time. He was humiliated. He had had it; he was through.

He lay there on the track, his hands covering his eyes, but he could still feel his father's look, "Get up, son, finish the race." The boy got up one last time and shot down the track, by now, far too behind to catch up, but he was going to finish the race.

The crowd cheered as the winner's chest broke the tape. But as the lagging boy hero finally came over the finish line, the crowd rose to its feet, and there was a thundering ovation. The father and son embraced. They were both crying.

"It's your best shot," Bonnie said. "That's what counts."

Curt looked softly at his wife. He smiled. "Marrying you is the best thing I ever did."

"Curt, you know the fact that we're here at all is like a victory," Bonnie said lovingly. "I'm really proud of you. I mean. . .I'm proud of you *already*."

He smiled again. "I'm proud of me, too." He really was, and he was amazed that he could relax the day before the race. He was usually all knotted up by this time.

That night in the hotel room, Curt watched *Rocky II* again. It was the same experience all over again, the same music pounded in his brain, and the same fighting spirit made his heart swell up. He slept well.

The next morning, Curt woke slowly; then it hit him that this was his day of reckoning. As he lay there, he worried about an insulin reaction if he took his shot early; he decided to chance it. Bonnie was hustling by now, and she infected Curt with her excitement. She was the best coach anybody ever had. Breakfast was eggs, sausages, and French toast, with orange juice and milk.

As they rode on the bus, Curt ate doughnuts and sucked on oranges. He had to keep his sugar level high through the race, and two and one-half hours of sustained muscle activity was a long time. He began to get nervous, but it wasn't that bad. He'd never felt this way before a race.

Finally they got to Hopkinton, a little town outside of Boston. Eight thousand runners were crammed into the little town, stretching, jogging, jazzed to the hilt; the air was jammed with the roar of their voices. A hot air balloon floated up into the clear blue sky. The day would be beautiful, maybe even warm.

Family and friends orbited the runners, holding warm-up suits, rubbing, encouraging. It was incredible. Curt felt a hot flush of excitement. This was his element. He could live off this energy every day of his life. Rocky's theme song began pounding in his brain again.

The wheelchair competitors moved over to the elementary school, one block away from the starting line. They were getting a little more solemn — nervous — checking their gear, spinning their wheels, making sure everything was right and tight. Curt put bandaids on each one of his fingers, then checked his two pairs of gloves. He looked up at the sun; it was warm — even hot, a perfect day for Wheelers. His friends were there, Dottie, Hugh, Kim, giving support. Curt felt a gentle touch on his shoulder. It was Bonnie, reminding him of the story about the boy and his dad, about getting back up and trying to win. Bonnie was more motivating in her quiet, soft way than anyone else could possibly be.

It was time to line up. The Wheelers were given a fifteen minute lead on the other runners. There were three lines of wheelchair competitors, and Curt found himself on the front line. Suddenly the gun went off, splitting the air and startling Curt into motion. His confidence was quiet and secure as his wheelchair sped ahead. "I'll go for it this year; I'll push hard."

Curt felt a surge of energy, and he rammed his arms downward, pushing like pistons, forcing the wheels around. Within twenty yards of the starting line, he found himself in second place, behind Jim Martinsen. It was an early lead, and it didn't mean anything yet — not unless he could go the distance. He pulled in behind Martinsen and "drafted" Jim the first 1¾ miles.

Much of the first leg of the race was downhill. The wheels whipped down the slope, picking up tremendous speed, frightening spectators along the road who unconsciously moved back. When Curt came in too close to Jim, he pulled out to the side, coasting until Martinsen pulled ahead, then he pulled in behind Jim to "draft" him again. Another mile went by. Curt gripped the wheels, rotating them quickly and powerfully, then let go, looking back to see who was close to him. Curt could see George Murray in his chair a quarter of a mile back. Curt sucked in his breath and thought aloud. "This is incredible. I'm going this fast, and I'm this far ahead of George Murray. Unbelievable!"

By now the "leg" runners had started.

Another two miles went by, Jim and Curt leading the pack of 8,000 marathoners. Curt still felt fresh and exhilarated, his sweat drying in the hot breeze almost as fast as his body could produce it. Curt coasted for a few seconds and took a long pull at his bottle of orange juice. The juice went down his throat, feeling cold and sweet, and it gave him a good lift.

The two leaders kept up their pace. At four miles, Curt began to feel a small stitch in his side. It started to get stronger and sharper, until he was really hurting, each stroke of the wheels making him double up, the cramps were so bad. He wondered how long he could keep this up.

Martinsen pulled away quickly as Curt lost momentum. He tried to push his wheels harder, but the harder he pushed, the more his side hurt. Something beside his cramps was making him sick. He groaned aloud. He had worked so hard, and he'd had such a tremendous start. To end this way was too frustrating. It was worse than if he'd never been a leader in the first place.

Curt limped along, sucking in his breath with each crippling pain, moving forward by sheer willpower. At the eight mile mark, he heard the familiar "whoosh, whoosh," behind him. It was George Murray, catching up. He whizzed past, and all Curt could do was watch Murray's back as he disappeared down the road. "Well, this is it," he said, bitterly. "Everyone will pass me now."

Somehow he kept going, watching ahead and faintly seeing George Murray pass Jim Martinsen at tremendous speed. Nine miles had gone by. He had seventeen miles to go, and he felt like somebody was stabbing him every time he moved. He kept asking himself if it was worth it. . .keeping this up. Then the pain started to ease up a little — then a little more. Curt cautiously tried to push harder; he didn't want the pain to rush him again. At ten miles the pain left him, and Curt leaned into his wheeling. He pushed and he pushed and started making tracks. Before long he caught sight of Jim Martinsen. After that, all he could see or think of was Jim; catch Jim, pass Jim. He was coming closer. People were cheering, screaming. He was now on Jim's tail, at his side, passing him. Suddenly Jim was behind, and Curt felt new strength, new desire.

His objective switched. It was George Murray now, a tiny speck in a tiny wheelchair, 500-600 yards ahead. Curt could see him, and he pushed his wheels with every bit of strength he had. If George was still in clear sight at eighteen miles, Curt had a good chance of catching him on Heartbreak Hill.

Once he had a solid game plan, Curt could relax. He concentrated all his strength and energy into each push, one at a time. His speed improved, and the tiny speck that was George Murray got bigger and bigger. He was sweating now, and it soaked his headband, stinging as it dribbled into his eyes. It ran down his back and under his buttocks, soaking into the wheelchair pad seat. For just a few seconds, he coasted and took a fast tug at the bottle, and the lukewarm liquid moistened his parched throat. Then he was off again, pushing in long, even strokes.

Now Heartbreak Hill came in sight. George Murray, still about 200 yards ahead, started up the steep incline, the nemesis of Boston Marathoners. If a runner could make it up that hill, he would finish the race.

The crowd lining the road was sparse at this point. They weren't expecting any marathoners this far this soon. In fact, no one had ever hit Heartbreak Hill so soon in the race. George and Curt were wheeling so fast, their time stunned even Curt. He knew, if they kept it up, they would come close to a two-hour race. It was phenomenal. The Boston record was two hours eight minutes thirty-five seconds, set by Derek Clayton, and he was a runner with legs. No Wheeler had ever beaten the leg runners in this race, ever. Curt was getting excited, but he didn't lose his efficiency or speed.

Because the crowd was so sparse, Curt had a lot of space to maneuver on the hill. During the other Boston Marathons, the crowd on the hill had seemed to close in on him, making him nervous and tightening him up. But not today. He felt strong, and confident, so he hauled himself up the extended hill faster than he ever had before. When he finally got to the top, Curt could see George only 80-100 yards ahead, close enough that Curt could catch him, and that's just what he meant to do. Now he had to make his play — he was about to run out of time.

He flew down the hill — his speed was incredible, but he was in total control. One mile went by, then two. George was now only forty yards away. Curt hit a sharp turn, and there were people shouting, "Catch him, catch him."

Policemen on horseback were battling to keep the crowd off the roadway. As Curt approached the mounted police, one horse reared, came down, and back up, almost plunging into Curt. But Curt just grabbed his wheel, veered sharply to the right, and blazed on down the road. Everything happened so fast he had no time to feel scared. He would have time for that later on.

Dead ahead were the Trolley tracks. They slanted right down the middle of the road here, and though they were no threat to the legged runners, they presented a formidable barrier to the Wheelers. Curt maneuvered between the tracks and kept up his speed. He wasn't sure what to do. If he crossed the tracks, he could lose a wheel or take a hard fall; he was going 25-30 miles per hour, way too fast for that kind of a jolt.

"What do I do?" he asked. "How am I going to get out of this? Can I ride it out to the bottom of the hill and not hit a track?" The typical Boston crowd usually closed in at this point, forcing the Wheelers across the tracks. But today it was too early for the big crowd, so Curt had space and time, and he chose to go right on down between the tracks to the bottom of the hill. By now, George, who was thirty yards ahead, had hit the bottom of the hill and was crossing the four sets of tracks at a sharp turn in the road. His speed and angle were too precarious; he hit one set of tracks wrong, and suddenly he crashed, falling out of his broken chair. As Curt watched, he winced and felt sorry for George. He really wanted to win but not by default. Curt watched George right his wheelchair and climb back in. When George began pushing himself slowly down the road, he looked as depressed as Curt guessed he must be. Those crummy tracks — right now, he and George should be sprinting, racing the last two miles to the finish line.

Curt was confident he could have caught George anyway, but the fall had taken the challenge right out of things — until Curt remembered Jim Martinsen. Where was he? Curt began pushing hard again, as though Martinsen were breathing down his neck. Curt meant to win; nothing was going to stop him now.

The two-mile sprint was on. But the twenty-four previous miles began to tell on him, and cramps tore at his chest and biceps. Each time Curt brought his arm back to grab hold of the rim, his bicep would cramp. Then, as he pushed out far to stretch the bicep, his chest would cramp. It was a see-saw torture. Curt felt almost crazy with pain, it was so hard to keep going. He could just see himself dying in the home stretch. Twice Curt had to use his left arm to straighten out his right arm.

He rounded the second to last corner, headed up Hereford Street for two hundred yards, then went into the final turn. People were going crazy, yelling and screaming, urging Curt on. His body was spent, screaming at him that it had enough, but the will to win was too strong. He had to keep going.

The roar of the crowd told Curt he was coming up to the finish line. People began to yell, "Murray's coming, here comes George Murray. He's gonna set a record."

Curt would never be able to describe the feelings he'd had at that moment; he knew he had it won. He came around the final corner, and as he glanced back, he could see no one, no Wheelers, no runners. His favorite word boomed inside his head, "Incredible!" The crowd was going crazy.

Bonnie Brinkman, back in the crowd around the finish line, heard them yell, "Murray's coming," and she struggled to get a good look at him. She studied the form in the chair. She found herself talking out loud, "That guy is too skinny to be George Murray. It's Curt, it's Curt!" She couldn't believe it — it sent a thrill through her like she'd never felt before in her life.

She stood there, stunned for a few seconds, then she decided she had to be at the finish line to greet Curt, she just *had* to be. Bonnie knew that only race officials were supposed to be on the finish line, but just then, the rules just didn't matter. They could go ahead and arrest her, but she had to be there. Bonnie pushed and shoved her little self through the crowd, then ran toward the finish line. A big man reached out and grabbed her arm, stopping her in mid-flight. She yelled out, "That's my husband down there," and yanked her arm back, surprising the big man with her strength.

As Curt wheeled across the finish line, he raised his arms high over his head and yelled, "It's my year, finally my year!" The roar of the crowd was deafening, but one little voice stood out from all the rest. Curt looked up, and there she was, the girl he loved. When she got to him, she nearly knocked him out of the chair in her excitement. Bonnie's eyes glowed with pride, and Curt was thrilled to have her there at his proudest moment.

Suddenly the loudspeaker boomed: "Ladies and gentlemen, the time of the first place winner of the wheelchair division, Curtis Brinkman, is one hour, fifty-five minutes." The crowd went wild again and with reason. Derek Clayton's 2:08:35 record had been shattered by some thirteen minutes! Curt had broken the wheelchair record by thirty-one minutes and had broken his own personal record by thirty-nine minutes. The effort had been phenomenal, especially because it was done by a young Utahn who was expected to do well by placing fourth or fifth, as the meet directors told Bonnie later. It was another historic day in Boston.

Underneath the pride of the moment, Curt was cramping badly. He was taken down the ramp leading beneath the Prudential Center and rolled toward the medical table where helpers rubbed his shoulders, got fluids down him, and checked his vital signs. Slowly he cooled down, and the pain subsided little by little. Finally, they got Curt into good enough shape to give interviews for the media. By that time, Bill Rogers, the leader of the runners, had come in — a full seventeen minutes *after* Curt's fifteen minute wheelchair "handicap."

The reporters wanted to know how Curt lost his legs, how he got into marathoning, and what his feelings were about his tremendous victory. He answered their questions and went on to talk about the upcoming Para-Olympics in Holland. The following article appeared in a Boston paper a day later:

BOSTON — Ten years ago, an Idaho schoolboy named Curt Brinkman climbed a power pole and lost both legs when an arc of electricity literally blew his knees off. Yesterday, Brinkman was the first person to finish the Boston Marathon.

Just one hour and 55 minutes after he left Hopkinton, Brinkman turned down the ramp leading beneath the Prudential Center and rolled toward the medical table. When Bonnie Brinkman saw that her husband had won the race, she burst out a scream of joy, then wept softly.

"We wanted this one so much," Bonnie said, wiping away the tears. "It's wonderful . . . amazing, fantastic. We found out a couple of months ago that Curt has diabetes. This is the first marathon we've attempted since he's been on insulin. It's fantastic."

It doesn't seem that anything can stop Curt Brinkman. Trage-

dies have been a part of his life — the terrible accident in the Idaho field and the discovery of diabetes.

He has been slowed momentarily by those ugly occurrences, but he cannot be stopped. Determination and drive have always prevailed, as was the case yesterday when Curt set a record. His 1:55 marked the first time anyone had ever completed the course in less than two hours; the old wheelchair record was George Murray's 2:26:05.

Brinkman puts his problems on the back burner and looks at the bright aspects of his life. He gets the most of everything he has, which is much. His bubbling personality is complemented by his midwestern politeness. The Brinkmans have two young children who were left back in Utah.

Bonnie and Curt were both winners yesterday afternoon.

Bonnie endured every inch of

the grueling, 26-mile, 385-yard trek with her husband — in her heart.

"She's been a big motivational factor to me," Curt said. "If you want to do well, you've got to put in a lot of time and determination. On those days when I didn't really want to go out, she'd say to me, 'Don't you want to go to Boston, don't you want to run in the marathon?'" Those subtle hints paid off yesterday.

"I think this year more than any has been rough for him," Bonnie said. "It's been really hard for him to train because his joints are wearing out. He really wanted it badly — worse than anything."

Brinkman, a 26-year-old Brigham Young graduate, trailed favored Murray for the first 23 miles, but Murray's wheelchair jammed into a trolley track and ruined a tire. He was forced to withdraw.

The hills which dot the marathon's course prove to be many a runner's downfall. That goes for the wheelchair athletes, too. The power in Brinkman's arms drove him up the long, rolling hills, but the tougher part for the wheelchair racer is going down the hills, when he must not lose control. Brinkman perfected that. He claimed he made his best time going up the steep grades, pushing along at a smooth, steady pace.

And, as a runner's most valuable piece of equipment is obviously his footwear, the wheelchair athlete's is obviously his wheelchair.

Brinkman claims to have had the heaviest chair of any of the contestants. Was the added weight to his advantage?

"All I know about it is that it has a lot of chrome on the side," he smiled. "I don't have the money to build it up. I won, though, so it's gotta be pretty good, doesn't it?"

The wheelchair, however, cannot take much of the credit. The man who piloted the vehicle over the potholes, beer bottles and trolley tracks deserves most of the praise. He and the wheelchair have logged between 100 and 200 miles a week since January.

"When I started training, I trained for this and only this," Brinkman said. "I wanted it more this year than any other year (this was his fourth Boston Marathon). I had to be more careful now, though, because of my (diabetic) condition. I had to have my sugar with me in case of an emergency.

"I just wanted to break 2:20," Brinkman said. "This was great, but I'm so glad it's over. It's been a tough weekend."

Back at the hotel and on the way home, Curt couldn't help but compare the news coverage the Wheelers got with the coverage the media gave the leg runners. It was a poor comparison — the Wheelers got the raw end. On the flight home, he expressed his feelings to Bonnie: "You know, it really isn't right. If you consider the fact that it wasn't so long ago people thought people in wheelchairs couldn't even do a mile, and now I do 26.2 miles in one hour and fifty-five minutes, it just isn't right for the media to ignore it. It's very disappointing.

"There are even some race directors who are saying that people in wheelchairs can't compete in the marathons. That's really a step backwards for society. I think it is too bad that there are people like that, who don't believe in helping people to build their self-esteem, their desire to go out and compete and live like normal people. It is really a sad thing for people not to recognize what good can come from this kind of accomplishment.

"Wheelchair competitors don't expect to be classified exactly the same as runners, but we want to have the same opportunities, the same thrills, and the same experiences. I really didn't expect anybody to say that I was the overall winner. Bill Rogers got that, and I think that's great; I think Bill Rogers is a fantastic person. But I do think the wheelchair competitors ought to receive more recognition, so they can go throughout the country, and not only help improve their own self-concept, but also motivate other people — not only other physically handicapped people, but also 'normal' people.

"I think what people like me can do can be a great inspiration for lots of normal people in all parts of their lives.

"I really feel bad about this, the people, the race directors, and the media who don't cover it that well. And I just think it shows a great lack of understanding as to what is going on and what can be accomplished."

Curt and Bonnie finally touched down in Salt Lake City, worn out but elated. They went up to Idaho to retrieve little Greg and Lorian, then headed home to Provo. Not long after they returned, the *Salt Lake Tribune* paid Curt and Bonnie this tribute:

The price of success didn't come cheaply for Curt Brinkman, but then sometimes it never does.

Brinkman, 26, a double amputee from Orem, two weeks ago wheeled across the finish line of the Boston Marathon in a world record time of one hour, 55 minutes to become the first wheelchair athlete to outpace the able-bodied runners.

Utah Gov. Scott Matheson has declared Monday "Curt Brinkman Day. . . ."

Brinkman has been going for it for years, and his victory in the Boston Marathon must rank as one of the top sports stories in Utah histories.

CHAPTER THIRTEEN
The Olympics

Soon after Bonnie and Curt came home from Boston, the World Olympiad for the Handicapped, the Para-Olympics in Holland became the big focus in their lives. The team wouldn't be leaving the U.S. until June 17, so Curt had some time to make his plans and get his money together. The money seemed like no problem at all this time. When the Brinkmans came home from Boston, the Utah Governor's Office had assured them that funds would be provided for the Holland trip.

Curt had been a little doubtful then as to whether he really wanted to go to Holland, but the Governor had said, "We want you to go, if that is your desire," and he gave Curt the promise of government support. With that kind of encouragement, Curt decided he would go, and he left the financial preparations to Utah while he got into shape.

In April, an administrative assistant was put in charge of Curt's project. As time went by, she assured Curt repeatedly that things were going well, that the funds were indeed being raised, and that he would have them in plenty of time.

There *was* a little time pressure on Curt. All of the American wheelchair athletes, and there were 96 of them including the amputee team and the coaches, needed to submit the money for their trip to Mr. Lipton, the chairman of the National Wheelchair Athletic Association, before they could actually secure their places on the team and the flight to Holland. So when it got to be two weeks before the departure date, and there had still been no money forthcoming, Curt called the assistant for the fourth time and she told him once again that everything was just fine, that he'd have the funds the very next week — the week before the trip.

A week later there was still no money. Curt finally had to call Mr. Lipton and tell him it didn't look like he could go after all. "Cancel my seat," he said, "and get somebody else." Then he called the assistant again to tell her the trip was off.

"Oh, no," she said. "You're for sure going." She persuaded him to call Mr. Lipton back, which he did. It turned out that because they'd had to cancel his seat on the flight, he'd lost the low fare he would have had as part of a pre-paid group, and the ticket would now cost $400 more. But they hadn't found someone to take his place on the team; there just hadn't been enough notice. Mr. Lipton told him that he could still go.

He called the lady to tell her about the additional $400, and she said that was fine, they would take care of everything for him. He called her every day, and every day she gave him the same answer — tomorrow. It was always tomorrow that the money would come. They finally got down to the wire; it was the day before Curt was to leave. The morning passed, and then the afternoon, and there were still no funds.

"This is it," Curt said miserably. "I guess I'm not going." It wasn't a happy day.

That afternoon Curt was doing some public relations for Stan Cottrell who was running across country and who, at the time, was just outside of Provo. In the course of the interview with Stan, the reporters asked Curt about Holland, eventually dragging the whole frustrating story out of him. They aired it on the six o'clock news; all of the stations had something about it, capitalizing on the drama in the fact that he was supposed to be leaving at nine o'clock the next morning.

As soon as the news people finished Curt's story and moved along to the weather, the calls began, and it wasn't long before Curt had the pledges he needed. One businessman from Salt Lake pulled up in front of Curt's place in a Lincoln Continental and peeled four one hundred dollar bills off a roll that looked big enough to finance the whole trip and then some. "Here," he said.

"I'm sick of the way big government fouls things up. If you need any more in the morning, you let me know. I'll make sure you get whatever you need."

There were others who met Curt at the airport the next morning, bringing money and good wishes, seeing him off. He flew from Salt Lake to New York, where he met Mr. Lipton, a small, reserved man who held a pipe in his hand, though he rarely smoked it. He greeted Curt and was very gracious about accepting the check.

There were sixteen members of the American amputee team, several of them double amputees. Jim Martinsen was there, just as he'd been in Boston, and the team also included Jim Finch, John Jerome, and Dickie Bryant.

The airplane that was to take them to Holland was one of the Royal Netherlands Airline's 747s. It was incredibly huge, and it presented an almost insurmountable difficulty for the wheelchair team members. Because there were few people there to help the team board, it was very slow going. The situation was embellished, not to say complicated, by the crowds of people at the gate, cheering for the team. The other passengers on the flight were scattered through the crowd, waiting until the team was all settled before they could board.

Finally, John Jerome, who weighed around two hundred pounds and who was not going to be carried by anybody, led his four comrades — Curt, Dickie, and the two Jims — down the ramp to the door of the plane, where he jumped out of his chair and scooted up the aisle on his hands, kind of "frogging" it to his seat. Curt laughed to himself, thinking how strange it had to look, five big heads, bobbing up and down, like a bunch of monkeys romping past the seats.

Once they got into the air, the trip was uneventful, except that Curt, because of his diabetes, found himself suffering from a fairly painful degree of hydraulic pressure, and finally after he had waited as long as he humanly could — had to scoot himself along to the bathroom four times, feeling mortified every time he had to do it.

They landed in Amsterdam fourteen hours after they'd left New York. They were tired. And the deplaning was difficult. The other passengers cheered the team as they bobbed back down the aisle, which was nice, but then there was the horrible confusion of the wheelchairs; there were over ninety wheelchairs that had to be dealt with, and everyone had to find his own chair before they could get anywhere.

The Red Cross stepped in to help, wanting to fetch the team in Red Cross chairs one by one, and then transfer each one to his own chair, but that only made for more confusion. So it was a long wait, and then confusion, and then more waiting. Finally, things got straightened out, and the team was loaded on a bus that took them from Amsterdam to the Olympic Village. It was an eighty mile trip, and it took an hour and forty minutes, an eternity for the already weary team. Curt kept a lookout for windmills, but he never got to see any from the bus. All he could see were the huge power lines that seemed to be strung everywhere. It was a little disappointing.

When they finally got to the game site, the American team found that the confusion had only begun. Curt was stuck away in the far end of a temporary barracks with a few members of the team who were strangers to him. This place was an addendum to the area that had been set aside for members of the Irish team. He wasn't excited about being there.

Some of the quadraplegics were uncomfortable in their bungalows because the places were unheated and would have been uncomfortable even for people whose circulation was normal, so they joined Curt's group, commandeering the beds that had not yet been claimed by the Irishmen.

Finally, Curt and Jim Finch found out that there were two extra beds where some of their buddies were staying, so they were moving their things to that new place just as the encroaching Americans were ejected from the Irishmen's quarters. Then things finally settled down a little.

The beds that Curt and Jim ended up with were bunk beds. Curt took the top one because it was easier for him to reach than it would have been for Jim. He sat up there on his bed, feeling good to be in a room with his friends, relieved that the ordeal of getting there was finished, and that the games would happen soon.

Suddenly, Rod Vleiger looked up at him from below and said, "What kind of wisdom do we have from the monk on high?"

Curt looked down at him, assuming a grave air, and answered, "Say your prayers, and you will win mightily." Everybody in the room cracked up. It was the first of many traditions the athletes would develop over the next three weeks.

Every morning after that, one of the guys would say, "Okay, what kind of advice do we have from the monk on high this morning?" It was all a big joke, of course. Nevertheless, they all knew that Curt was a Mormon, and they had some respect for his beliefs, so he took the opportunity to slip in some real advice once in a while. Most of the members of the team were good married men, fun, but not unruly, and the three weeks they had to spend away from home wasn't going to be easy for a lot of them, so Curt threw out an occasional scripture, and the rest of the guys grew to appreciate it. In fact, those few serious times went a long way towards cementing the team, making them more patient.

They were a good bunch of guys. There were only a few who smoked, and they were kind enough to do it outside of the quarters. There were a few who liked late nights and spent a good deal of time at the huge beer tent in the middle of the grounds, talking, laughing, and drinking until sometimes as late as one or two in the morning. Curt's group went to bed early as a rule, and sometimes the noise outside was disturbing.

Every morning Curt got up at six-thirty or so to eat breakfast. Then he headed back to bed and stayed there until nine or nine-thirty when the rest of the group finally got up. They had arrived a few days early, so that the team could settle in and get used to things before they had to deal with the pressure of the competition, and that was a very good thing for Curt because his two main events were to be run on the first two days of the games.

His first race was the hundred meter dash. The other members of the team had been giving Curt a hard time about his chair. "Boy," they'd say, "how are you going to have a chance in that heavy piece of furniture of yours?" He let it get to him. He started trying out everyone else's chair, looking for something lighter, something to give him a better edge.

Just before the race, he decided he would try Jim Finch's chair; it was light, but he wasn't feeling comfortable in it. It was too short in the seat, so Curt couldn't push down on it to get the leverage he needed when he tried to bear down on the wheels. He used it anyway.

They lined up to start, and Curt was already regretting his choice. The chair just didn't feel natural to him. The gun went off, and Curt got a very slow start. Even so, before he knew what had happened, he found himself in second place, coming right up on Jim Martinsen, who was leading the field.

In the end, Jim edged Curt out of first place by only 45/100 of a second; it was very close. Curt could have kicked himself, knowing he could have won the race if he'd just put out a little more. He felt a little better with the silver, though, when he saw how much good getting the gold medal had done for Jim.

The next race was the four hundred meter. Curt wasn't too hot about using Finch's chair again, but he still didn't want to use his own, so he tried out Brad Parks'. It was actually not a whole lot better, but Curt decided to use it anyway. The four hundred was very important to him; he wanted to win it more than he wanted anything just then. It was the last individual race Curt was going to participate in, and he was determined about the outcome.

They lined up to start, and Curt suddenly felt discouraged, pretty much conceding the race to Jim Martinsen in his heart. The starter yelled, "Op your plosson," instructing everyone to take their seat, and it cracked up the whole line. They wouldn't have been there *without* their seats. Then the gun went off.

Jim Martinsen was out in front like a flash. Curt was pulling up close, wanting to beat him so bad, he was pushing hard. The other competitors just weren't strong enough to catch them, so there they were, the two of them, Curt on the inside, and Jim in the second lane, nobody else closer than several chair lengths behind. They came around the corner, and Curt pulled up so that the front edge of his chair was about even with the back of Jim's. Jim slowed a little, and so did Curt, knowing he had a good lead on the field, and they had a little breather.

They were doing the last part of the corner when Curt decided to make his move. He had been waiting for Jim to make his, but Jim hadn't changed pace, so Curt took off, pushing it very hard, and passed him. He could just feel Jim coming up behind, and he pushed even harder. When he crossed the finish line, he had several chair lengths on Jim, and he had won the gold.

Later on, Martinsen said that he had tried to catch Curt, that he'd pressed as hard as he could, but he just couldn't get it together to go like Curt had gone.

It was an exhilarating moment for Curt, being awarded a gold medal, seeing the pride in the faces of his friends. And now the pressure was off for awhile. He had two more events to go, the two relays, and lawn bowling. He was a little worried about lawn bowling; he hadn't done it for awhile, and he was going to be competing against people who were trained, but he figured he'd do his best when the time came. The time was two weeks away. Those events were to take place on the last day of the competition, so Curt and Jim had fourteen days open.

They saw everything there was to see in the immediate area, and there was quite a lot of activity going on. They found a carnival, actually more of a fair, at Popendahl outside the Olympic games, where they found steelcraftsmen who did beautiful work, barrelmakers, and wooden-shoe makers. They talked to people they met there, sampling the character of the country.

After taking in the local sights in just a few days, Curt and Jim were getting impatient sitting around. "We've *got* to do something with the time we've got left," Jim exclaimed.

They had casually kicked around the idea of wheeling to Amsterdam. Now they were thinking that it wouldn't be a bad trip. They got hold of a map of the bicycle paths that criss-crossed Holland, and they carefully planned a route. They recruited one of the hostesses, Margaret, who could speak both English and Dutch, and they made very careful plans, taking packs full of food and extra tubes and tires. They were planning to do the whole eighty miles, so they had to be careful about their preparation.

When the big morning dawned, Jim was ready to go before Curt had any breakfast. It wouldn't have been so bad, except that Curt had just had his insulin, and doing that kind of work on no food was very difficult for him. They did five miles, and Curt couldn't get up any speed. Jim was crazy to get going, just like he always was. Finally, Curt had to stop and explain the situation.

While they were stopped, Curt ate some of the honey he'd brought along as instant energy, and Jim gave him a little carton of orange drink. They started off again, but Curt was still having trouble.

They had started that morning without their guide. She just didn't get up in time, so they'd left without her. It wasn't long before she caught up with them. It turned out that she had jumped on her bike and sped out to find them, going the wrong direction. She had to ride all over before she finally located them, and when she did, she rode up behind them like she was a private detective or something.

From that point on, Margaret accompanied them on bicycle which was what they had planned originally, and which, after the exuberance of her arrival, seemed the safest thing.

They passed through beautiful country, and Curt finally got to see his windmills. He also had a flat tire, but as they had been prepared for such a contingency, it wasn't any real problem. They stopped at a garage for some pop and had a good talk with the folks that worked there. They were invited in for coffee, but after they explained that they didn't drink coffee, the owner of the place cheerfully sent them on their way with several hours' worth of pop instead.

At lunch time they stopped in a little park across from the Queen's palace. Eating like true continentals, the feast consisted of raisins, peanuts, oranges, bread, and cheese. While eating, they took in the splendor of the Queen's grounds. After some good old American picture taking, they headed on down the road again, refreshed by both the food and the beauty of what they had seen.

They passed through a number of cities on their way, and Margaret was a great help to them, asking directions, and leading them through the streets with virtually no problem at all. It was well into the afternoon when they saw the sign "Amsterdam — 42 kilometers," which told them they had only about twenty-six more miles to go.

"Hey, Jim," Curt yelled. "Only a marathon left!" They were getting a little tired, and it was exciting to them, knowing exactly what it would take for them to finish the trip. They had already done fifty to sixty miles that day.

They passed green fields and canals. There were gardens and flowers and water everywhere, and the country seemed lit up with reflections of brilliant color.

As they got closer to Amsterdam, the trees thinned, and the land leveled out. The city was close to the ocean, so the wind began to whip around them, smelling of brine, getting stronger as they went, sometimes gusting against them at thirty miles an hour. It made for hard wheeling. The going was easier for Margaret on her bike, so she took the lead, and Curt and Jim took turns "drafting" her.

Curt's left arm was giving him trouble again. It got so bad that when they stopped for short rests, he could hardly get going again. But he made it to the city. They were just entering Amsterdam when they had to stop at a raised bridge. They watched the boat pass slowly by, and they talked with a group of people on bicycles.

The bikers wondered what they were doing, and when the Wheelers told them about it, no one would believe them. It took

Margaret to convince them, and then they were utterly amazed.
"You guys must be something else," they said. "Eighty miles in wheelchairs." By then, the bridge had been lowered, so they parted company, and the two Wheelers and their guide stopped for a drink and a rest at a small cafe.

When they got out on the road again, Jim wanted to sprint into town, but Curt's arm was so bad he could hardly limp along. Jim just shot on ahead, and Margaret began to feel concerned. She didn't want to leave either of the young men alone, and she took up a position somewhere between them so she could keep track of both.

Curt finally got up a good rhythm, and the pain in his arm subsided a little, but he still wasn't in racing shape. He caught Jim at every light; then the light would change and Jim would take off again, and that's the way it was until they finally got into the middle of town where the road circled back on itself, bordering a huge fountain that was the center of the city. Here Jim got a flat tire, and they had to change the wheel completely before they could go any further.

Curt about had it by then. "Look," he said, "let's find the hostel and get a shower and some sleep." Just then Jim pointed. There were some Olympic buses coming down the street. The German and Italian teams had decided to do some sight-seeing, and they were just on their way back to the Olympic Village. Margaret talked to one of the drivers while his team was looking at the fountain, and she finally convinced him to take the two Americans back with him.

As Curt and Jim loaded themselves on the bus, Jim said he could sure enjoy a Big Mac, so Margaret jumped right off and went to get him one. A little time went by, and the teams reloaded. "Time to go," the driver said, and Margaret wasn't back yet. Her bike was on the back of the bus, so as it slowly began to pull away from the curb, Curt and Jim worried for her.

Just as the bus completed its circle around the fountain, there was Margaret, doing a hundred-yard sprint. She made it.

The bus ride home was quiet. Curt found that he felt

awkward with Margaret, now that they had to sit quietly together. He didn't know her very well, and he was suddenly feeling the cultural distance between them. But Jim was fine. Jim could make conversation with anyone, anywhere, and Curt admired him for it.

When they got back to the bungalow, Curt jumped into the shower and stayed there for an hour and a half. Then he went straight to bed. He slept very well that night, and he felt great the next day, even though his arm still bothered him. He had four days to rest up before the last races. It was then that the trouble finally caught up with them.

Most of the coaches that had accompanied the American team really didn't do much in the way of athletic coaching. There were exceptions like Joe Gomez, but it was hard for even the good ones to advise someone in a wheelchair. So most of them just did a lot of chaperoning, loading and unloading, and keeping track of things, and evidently, one of them felt that Curt and Jim had taken too much liberty, going to Amsterdam the way they had without consulting him about it. So he went to the head coach, Cy Bloom, with a complaint.

Curt and Jim were instructed to get over to the team center and talk to Cy, but they weren't told why. The first thing Cy told them was that he was going to suspend them. He explained that they had been irresponsible, that they hadn't taken into account the affect their trip would have on the other athletes.

He asked them if they had anything to say. Curt was angry. In his mind, he flashed through a hundred arguments about how carefully planned the trip had been, how they'd taken a guide who could speak the language, even how the other athletes and coaches had thought the trip had been a great thing, but he could see that Cy had his mind made up and that no amount of talk would make a difference, so he didn't say anything and neither did Jim.

The severity of the punishment seemed to have shocked the coach who had brought complaint against them in the first place, and later he would write a letter to the National Committee stating that suspension was too harsh, that these were two otherwise responsible athletes. But at that point, the damage was done. The only good thing about it was that the suspension couldn't actually be brought into effect until after the games, so Curt and Jim could participate in the last events.

The news got around, of course. Everyone wanted to know what had happened. Curt made it a policy not to say any more than he had to. He knew that Cy was a hard worker and that he donated a lot of time to the Wheelchair Association, so Curt didn't want to see the other athletes come down on him.

The next few days passed slowly, and Curt found it hard to sleep at night. He was still worried about the lawn bowling, and you could never tell about relays; you had to depend so heavily on other people in that kind of event.

Finally, the last day of competition dawned, and the games began. The American team participated in the hundred meter relay first, won it easily, and Curt had his first gold medal of the day. Then he went up to the lawn bowling competition. It wasn't as difficult as he had expected it would be, and he was amazed when he realized that he was going to compete in the finals.

His last match was against an Egyptian who smiled warmly at Curt and then proceeded to tell him how many other people he had beaten in international competition. He had won the Stoke-Manville games, which were the first games ever held for wheelchair athletes. The Egyptian shrugged, "I guess I'm just that good," he said.

But Curt beat him anyway. The score at the end of the match was twenty-one to seven. It was Curt's third gold medal, the second that day. After that match, he barely had time to get ready for the big one, the four hundred meter relay.

The American team was a fast one, but it had one potentially weak point, Dickie Bryant. He wasn't a racer. He was more of a fieldman, a marksman. But the other three on the team, Curt, Jim Finch, and Jim Martinsen, were counting on him to perform, and perform he did. They beat the other teams hands down. And that meant four gold medals for Curt Brinkman.

No one could blame the American team for being proud. It was so good to live in a country where a man could pick up the pieces of his life and be productive, even after a devastating thing like losing both legs. Curt couldn't help but think about Russia, where the Olympics could have taken place, if it hadn't been for the fact that the Russians had declined, denying that they had any handicapped people. He had even heard that the Russians shipped everyone who was old or disabled out of Moscow for the regular Olympics, trying to convince the world that there were no imperfections in the people of Russia, as if being handicapped were something to be ashamed of.

Curt thought of the American difference and smiled. It was good to have a chance to be a man, even a man in difficult circumstances. And it was good to know that other countries gave their people the same chance. It was good to have the chance to be a winner, and with one silver medal and four gold, that's definitely how Curt was feeling.

Time finally arrived to go home. Of course, the departure had to be as confusing as the arrival had been. First it was the luggage. "Pack," the officials said. "We'll have you out of here in no time." But then, plans would change. "Unpack," they would say, shrugging. So the team would unpack and get ready to go see a few more things before they left, but they no sooner got out the door when someone would tell them to pack again, and that's how it went until they actually did leave.

Once they finally got to Amsterdam, there were more hitches, and getting home turned out to be a long, slow process: waiting here, waiting there, waiting at the airport, having to convince the airlines that the Red Cross didn't need to load each athlete, one at a time. Finally they got off the ground.

In New York, Curt was a little misinformed as to his reservations and only caught the right plane into Denver by accident. "Wow," Joe Gomez said, shaking his head as they boarded that flight together with Wes Brownlow, "Sure glad someone was here to babysit Brinkman."

It started out to be a very pleasant trip. The three of them relaxed and had a good talk about the games and about Curt's possible suspension. But before they got to Chicago, there was trouble with the plane, so they had to land, deplane, and wait an hour for another flight. Curt was concerned that he would miss his connection in Denver, and that's just what happened. They got into Denver an hour later than they should have, and Curt's flight to Salt Lake had already left.

"It's okay," Joe said. "You come stay with me. I'll get you here in time for your flight tomorrow morning." Curt was grateful, but he declined, and the airline put him up in a motel close to the airport. When he got settled into the motel, it was one-thirty in the morning, and it had been a good three days since he had any sleep to speak of.

He called Bonnie so she'd know what was going on; then he watched T.V. for awhile, too tired to fall asleep. Talking to Bonnie had only made things worse. He was tired, and he wanted to be home, not all alone in some motel, feeling like a stranger — which was exactly what he was in Denver.

Other places, he was Curt Brinkman, the man who won the Deseret News Marathon, or the man who won the Boston Marathon, or the man who won four gold medals in international competition, but in Denver at that moment he was only a very tired looking person in a wheelchair, and no one really cared who he was or where he had been. It was an empty, lost feeling, and he was very glad when the morning came so he could go get some breakfast and start home.

CHAPTER FOURTEEN
Discovery

When Curt finally disembarked in Salt Lake, Paul James of KSL-TV and Reese Stein of KUTV met him. There were cameras and interviews and cheering from the crowd assembled there. It was nice to know that people were there for him, but the best part of it was Bonnie, his own proud little wife, standing there by the kids waiting for him and looking like she was waiting for the other half of her heart to come back home.

It had been a long haul, the trip, and the hassle getting home. And when he finally did get home, the calls kept coming in, "Congratulations!" "Welcome home," "How does it feel. . . ." The weeks that followed were just as busy. Requests for appearances and speaking engagements kept rolling in until Curt finally had to start turning people down. He was just too busy with his church work to be able to answer every request. He was a member of the bishopric of the BYU 80th ward now, and he took that responsibility very seriously.

Another thing that was keeping him incredibly busy was his new job. Before he had left for Holland, he had worked for Deseret Industries as the assistant sales manager for their Provo store. When he told them about Holland, they told him they wanted him to open and manage a new store for them, but they would gladly give him the time he needed for the trip. He felt like they had been understanding and far more generous than he could have expected an employer to be, so now that he was back, he was working hard, trying to let them know how much he appreciated the way they had dealt with him.

So he was a busy man. And he was a tired man. And as time

went on and things only got busier, Curt found that he was a little confused as to what his priorities should be. His athletics were so important to him; they had been his strength and pride for so long now, but he couldn't give them the total attention they needed and still take care of the ward and his job. "Where is my life going?" he sometimes asked himself. "I need to concentrate on the important things."

It was during one of those nice, rare evenings when he had a chance to sit home quietly that things began to be a little more clear for him. He had been less than lively at dinner that night, and once when he looked at Bonnie, he had caught her appraising him a little worriedly. She had shrugged then and said, "You've been a little low spirited lately, I think."

"I don't know," he replied. "Bonnie, I just think maybe I am a little frightened about what to do next."

After dinner, Curt was sitting on the couch, trying to get into a book but not getting any farther than watching Greg and Lorian play on the floor, when Bonnie was suddenly sitting beside him, her arms full of unorganized folders.

"What have you got?" he asked, even though he knew.

"Your clippings. I just felt like looking them over might be kind of fun tonight." She opened the top folder and took out the first article she saw. "Look at that," she said, pointing to the picture. "Look what a hunk of a man I married." Curt laughed.

"The way I've got my arms up in the air all the time in those pictures you'd think I was a bird or something."

"Look, Curt," she said, "this was really a nice article." They read for awhile; then Bonnie pointed out a paragraph. "'Angler, camper, river-runner, horse-back rider, eagle scout, mountaineer,' that's a lot of things for one person to be," she said. Then she pointed to another paragraph. "'Brinkman said, 'I'd like to work with physically handicapped kids. The biggest problem with handicapped people is getting them to accept themselves. I want to show them they can do lot of things. They just don't know what they can do until they do it.'" She looked up at Curt and smiled.

"I've got to go get the kids ready for bed," she said. "I just want you to know — I want you to remember — you can do anything, Curt. Anything you decide to do. I love you." Then she was gone, taking the kids with her, and Curt was alone.

He looked through the clippings a little while longer, and as he did, he felt the old familiar pleasure he got out of feeling like a competitor, a winner. He hefted the folders in his hand. They were fat and heavy and full of clippings. "It really is amazing," he said to himself, "that all these things were done by a person with no legs. I sure wouldn't have believed it if they'd told me at the beginning I could do all this. I never thought I'd be able to do anything. In fact, I thought I was going to be a freak all my life. And instead, I turn out to be kind of famous."

The more he read the more he felt that he was Somebody, and he sat back and remembered how it had felt to get that fourth gold medal. He could hear the cheering and the bedlam, and it made him smile to himself. "I *can* do anything I want," he mused. He looked down at the clipping on top of the pile in his lap, and he saw the picture they had taken of him with Stan Cottrell, the man who had run across the United States, and he began to get excited.

"That's it," he said. "Nobody's every done that in a wheelchair. That's it. I'm going to wheel all the way across the country!" He put the folders down and leaned back, and just for fun went through the awards ceremony one more time. "It feels good to be famous," he said remembering. "It's important. . . ."

Then, suddenly, he remembered the stop-over in Denver on the way home from Holland. He remembered how he had felt after he had talked to Bonnie on the phone. "I was the same person that night in Denver as I was when I crossed the finish line at the Boston Marathon, but in Denver, Boston didn't seem to make any difference." He was on the verge of seeing something, just on the verge. "I was a successful person, but it didn't make me feel happy when I was alone there. It didn't fill me up. I was alone and empty anyway."

He thought about how much better he had felt when he got

off the plane in Salt Lake. The reporters and the news guys had all been there at the gate, and there had been a small group of people who were there to cheer him home, but those weren't the things that had made him feel better. It had been the sight of Bonnie and the kids. It had been Bonnie standing there that had made him feel like a whole man. And finally he saw through to the center of his confusion.

He put his hand on the folders. These things are nice, and managing the store is nice. Being in the bishopric is one of the greatest things that has ever happened to me. But Bonnie is what's important, Bonnie and Greg and Lorian. That's where my life is going. That's where my life will always, always be.

Someone dropped something heavy on his lap, and there was Lorian, grinning up at him. "Kiss your daddy goodnight," Bonnie said. Curt kissed Lorian, and then Greg scrambled up on the couch for a kiss. Curt put his arms around the children and looked up over their heads at his beautiful wife.

She smiled.

Mike Johnson and Curt training together at the Brigham Young University stadium.

Young people have meant a lot to Curt. In 1977 the children at Scera Park Elementary School in Orem, Utah raised funds for Curt and Mike Johnson in order for them to travel and compete in their first regional competition.

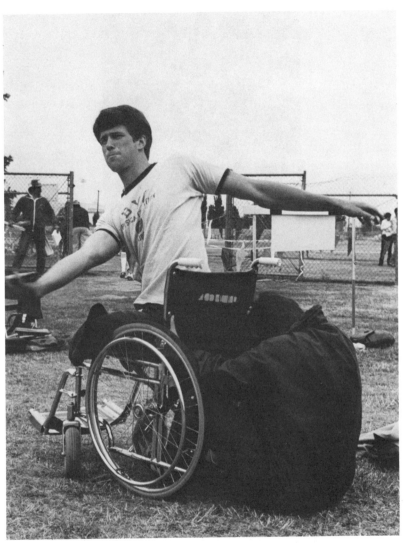

Curt threw the discus 114 feet here to win a medal in the 1977 National Tournament in California.

Curt proudly displays medals won in the Denver races in 1979.

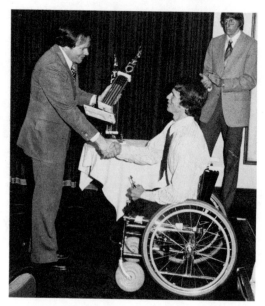

1978 Boston Marathon Awards Banquet — second place trophy — Wheelchair Division.

"The Golden Key" Award for exemplary achievement was presented to Curt Brinkman in 1977 by Utah Governor Scott Matheson in special ceremonies held in his honor.

His first Boston Marathon race, Curt garnered second place in the Wheelchair Division in 1977.

The start of the 1980 Boston Marathon, Wheelchair Division. Curt Brinkman won first place in the prestigious race and set a world's record.

One silver and four gold medals were awarded to Curt Brinkman at the end of the international Para-Olympic games in Holland, August 1980.

Provo, Utah mayor Jim Ferguson and other city officials become "Wheelers" for awhile in festivities held honoring Curt.

Shaking hands with well-wishers after the "Curt Brinkman Day" ceremonies in Utah County, Utah, Summer 1980.

Shown here with wife, Bonnie, Curt was honored as the Grand Marshall for the 1980 B.Y.U. Homecoming Parade and game.

The Curt Brinkman Family. They currently reside in American Fork, Utah.